MAFIA
PRINCESS

MARISA MERICO

with Douglas Thompson

THE EXPLOSIVE
TRUE STORY OF A BRITISH

MAFIA
PRINCESS

THEY'RE LAWLESS. THEY'RE CRIMINAL.
THEY'RE FAMILY.

HarperCollins*Publishers*

HarperCollins*Publishers*
77–85 Fulham Palace Road,
Hammersmith, London W6 8JB

www.harpercollins.co.uk

First published by HarperCollins*Publishers* 2010

3

A catalogue record of this book is
available from the British Library

ISBN 978-0-00-733203-8

Printed and bound in Great Britain by
Clays Ltd, St Ives plc

FOR LARA AND FRANK

'*The family – that dear octopus from whose tentacles we never quite escape nor, in our inmost hearts, ever quite wish to.*'

DODIE SMITH,

I CAPTURE THE CASTLE, 1948

'*But I don't want to go among mad people,*' *Alice remarked.*
'*Oh, you can't help that,*' *said the Cat:*
'*We're all mad here. I'm mad. You're mad.*'
'*How do you know I'm mad?*' *said Alice.*
'*You must be,*' *said the Cat. '*Or you wouldn't have come here.*'

LEWIS CARROLL,

ALICE'S ADVENTURES IN WONDERLAND, 1865

CONTENTS

FOREWORD

'Dream as if you'll live for ever, live as if you'll die today.'

JAMES DEAN, 1954

They shot dead my godfather with a 7.63 calibre pistol as he sat in his favourite barber's chair waiting for a wet shave.

An explosive bullet from a high-precision rifle blew the top off my dad's cousin's head as he left his house, in the hurried moment between his front door and his armour-plated car.

An uncle of mine was gunned down by automatic fire as he was serving wine in his café-bar one lunchtime.

Soon after, the man who issued the orders for these murders was killed while in protective custody, as he took his Sunday morning exercise in the prison yard. A marksman aiming from a building outside the prison walls put a rifled, explosive bullet in his forehead.

With nearly seven hundred combatants and innocents already dead, the violence was escalating every day and my family was suffering. Which was why, at the age of nineteen, I agreed to drive South with a consignment of military weapons packed into the secret compartments of the family's customised Citroën, the one that was usually used to traffic heroin.

We stacked machine pistols, handguns and rifles, clips of ammunition, bullet-proof vests and jackets on top of the heavier hardware: Kalashnikovs, those awesome AK-47s which can spray out 650 rounds a minute, and bazookas that toss armour-plated vehicles into the sky.

It was like packing your sweaters and skirts first in a holiday suitcase, having all the ironed stuff lying flat, your toilet bag and shoes stashed in the corners.

I was too young to understand the complexity of everything that was happening, and too dizzily in love with the boyfriend who came with me to feel scared – even when the *carabinieri* stopped for a chat alongside our car, where we had stashed away enough weaponry to start World War Three.

We didn't have a fear in the world. It was just like going on a family summer holiday.

After our delivery, the war became even more intense. The rival families didn't have the contacts to get military weapons like the Yugoslav bazookas we'd brought. Hit squads operated as four-men units: a driver, a shooter with a 12-gauge automatic Benelli, renowned in the lethal mechanics of urban warfare, two men with machine pistols. Russian RPGs, the antitank grenade launchers, were around. There were also arson teams to burn out the rivals who were taken down by rifle fire as they struggled to flee the flames.

Still it wasn't all one way. Uncle Domenico – a lovely, lovely man, full of laughter and fun, my Nan's brother, one of my favourite uncles – was shot dead as he strolled onto his bedroom balcony to smoke a cigar.

How many people have relatives who are shot and killed? I grew up with it.

These were insane times.

It was violence against violence and even then it was clear to me that the winner is the one who has the more homicidal equipment. And intentions.

I've learned such things for, even before I was born, violence was vital to my life.

It got me born.

CHAPTER ONE
GUCCI GUCCI COO

Fidarsi è bene, non fidarsi è meglio.
[To trust is good, not to trust is better.]

ITALIAN SAYING

I was born on my Nan's kitchen table. I emerged reluctantly, just in time for breakfast, in the middle room of her house in the Piazza Prealpi in Milan.

It was the same table on which my Nan had given birth to her twelve children, including her youngest, Angela, who'd arrived just four weeks earlier.

My mum didn't have any contractions. She was taking her time to deliver me and Nan's household wasn't used to that.

'Push! Push, push!' Nan's friend Francesca the midwife shouted at her.

Mum wasn't pushing, not at all. She didn't know what all the fuss was about. She was in a haze. She had no energy left. She'd been in labour for more than twelve hours.

'Go on, push!'

Nan couldn't understand the delay. When she'd given birth to Angela the month before, the production line had been as smooth as ever. This silly English girl on the kitchen table just didn't have a clue how to have babies. Shouting wasn't helping. The family had been up most of the night; they wandered around, yawning, trying to stay alert, but the coffee had stopped working hours before.

Now, at 8 a.m. on Thursday the 19th of February 1970, they'd had enough. Certainly my grandpa Rosario Di Giovine had. He wanted his breakfast.

'Nothing's happening, nothing at all,' said Nan.

Grandpa rolled up his sleeve: 'Right, come on! Come on, my girl ... *Vai! Vai!*'

He gave Mum a real slap on the leg. Then another, harder, on the backside: 'Come on – let's have you.'

Mum pushed.

I arrived at 8.09 a.m.

Grandpa went off to eat, as if nothing had happened. My nan went to a cupboard at the side of the room. The midwife swaddled me in cotton cloths, and Nan returned with a purple cashmere Gucci blanket, a gift from an associate, and wrapped me up in it.

It was appropriate. I'd been born into the Mob. I was a Mafia Princess.

My mum didn't have a lot of milk, so Nan breastfed me a few times. I loved my nan. I was always her favourite. Yet that Gucci blanket was no glass slipper. My early life was more like Cinderella's *before* the prince came on the scene. And certainly no fairytale.

As I grew up, the family were ferociously pursuing their business, and that involved a great deal of guns and drugs and death. For my father's family it had always been that way.

Nan was a pure bloodline Serraino, born in Reggio Calabria to one of the legendary 'Ndrangheta clans that make up the Calabrian Mafia. Pronounced *en-drang-ay-ta,* it translates as honour or loyalty, and loyalty to the family (or *'ndrina*) is in the blood, flowing through their veins.

Nan can't sign her name – she uses an X on documents – but she is one of the most remarkable Mafia figures of the past few decades, known widely as *La Signora Maria,* the Lady Maria. The authorities are ever so complimentary about her. I've seen Italian legal paperwork that ranks her the most dangerous woman in Italy.

I was named after her – Maria Elena Marisa (Di Giovine) – but people always called me Marisa; to avoid confusion, they said. Confusion? That was a good one. *La Signora Maria* is unique.

You don't join the 'Ndrangheta; your membership is ordained. All Nan's children knew the laws of such an indigenous and territorial Mafia family. They saw it as kids in Calabria, where my nan learned the gospel of violence first hand. People think that men run everything in the Mafia and the little woman isn't even allowed to stir the pasta sauce. About half an hour's sail across the Strait of Messina in Sicily, home of the Cosa Nostra, female roles were more like those you see in the movies, but in Calabria's 'Ndrangheta, built for more than 150 years on the blood family, women have always been heavily involved in both the kitchen and the crime. There are even sisters in *omertà* – the Mafia code of silence. There are stories of initiation ceremonies for women not born into the family to be formally accepted. Blood relations and family ceremonies such as weddings, communions, christenings and funerals, are the core of the life. And death. There wasn't ever a grey area with my nan. Nothing ambiguous about *La Signora Maria*.

She was the boss, the ultimate law.

And Pat Riley from Blackpool's mother-in-law.

Mum was a stunner – blonde, shapely and fun to be around – but brought up in the suburbs of north-west England to be practical and sensible. Up to a point. She's always been determined, her own person. The Blackpool Illuminations were never going to be the only bright lights in her life.

Patricia Carol Riley is a baby boomer, born on 17 January 1946, a little more than a year after her father, Jack Riley, returned from his wartime service in the ambulance corps. He and Grandma Dorothy had two more daughters, Gillian and Sharon. Granddad worked as a greengrocer, and Grandma had two jobs, one in a grocery store and another at the local Odeon. The long hours finally allowed them to buy themselves out of a council estate and into their own home for the sum of £3,000.

A treat for the girls was salmon paste sandwiches and tea on the beach next to Blackpool Promenade. It was a good life but quiet, ordinary. There were never going to be any surprises. It's easy to understand that it got boring for a bright teenager like my mum.

She has her artistic side, she has an 'eye'. She's absolutely brilliant at art. She's got an 'A' level in it and could have taught it but her dad wouldn't let her go to art college. He thought it would be a waste of time – a degree and then she'd be off to get married and have kids. He and my grandma just wanted husbands, not complications, for their girls.

Mum was fed up. She liked her job as a window dresser for Littlewoods in Blackpool but she felt she was going down a predictable road, which she had to somehow turn off. As Monday to Friday rolled along she felt more and more trapped. She had a *nice* boyfriend: Alan, tall, good-looking and someone you could take home to fish fingers for tea. It wasn't hot passion. When Alan started talking marriage, the alarm bells went off. There had to be something more, hadn't there? Brenda, her best pal, had found that working as an au pair in America. Or so she said in her many gossipy blue airmail letters about the boys and the wild nights out.

'America? Never!' screamed Grandma Dorothy. 'What's wrong with life here? It's good enough for the rest of us.'

But it wasn't for Mum. She felt she'd been nowhere, done nothing. And, strangely, she didn't *belong*. She was searching for something that she, never mind her mum and dad, couldn't understand. She dismissed her parents' predictions that she'd be bored and homesick. But she respected them enough to compromise about going to America. She read an advertisement in the *Lancashire Evening Post* placed by an Italian company that employed English au pairs. The catch was she had to get to Italy to get the job. Her mum and dad reluctantly gave their blessing – Italy was better than flying across the Atlantic – and after eleven long weeks of Saturday night telly, spending nothing, going nowhere, she had the fare to Milan.

'Our Gracie', her Nan's favourite old-time singer Gracie Fields, who'd been born over a fish 'n' chip shop in Rochdale, Lancashire, now lived in Capri. That was Italian! It was all very well to go to America, she thought, but at least with Europe it would be easier to get back home if she hated it. She arrived at Milan's Malpensa Airport with thirty pounds, not one word of Italian, and the astonishing high hopes and optimism of a twenty-one-year-old Lancashire lass.

She was a sensation. In 1967, blonde English girls were still something of a novelty. And she had an instant friend, Ada Omodie, who was eighteen years old and the eldest of the four children she'd been hired to look after. They were soon in a bartering relationship: Pat helped Ada with her English and Ada taught Pat Italian.

It was *La Dolce Vita*. Pat and Ada would go shopping together, and she went on holiday with the Omodie family to Rimini where they had their own villa. Guests included Giovanni 'Gianni' Rivera, a star of AC Milan and the Italian national soccer team. And Pat attracted as much attention as the celebrities at the swimming pool parties. It was something she was getting used to. The Omodie family lived in central Milan and there would be lots of wolf whistles as she walked the kids to school each day, even more when she wandered home on her own. She looked straight ahead, ignored everyone.

Except Alessandro.

He was the lot, the Trinity, tall, dark and handsome: he had an angelic face, like a Renaissance painting from her art books. Pat fell head over heels when she spotted him standing in the doorway of the barber's shop where he worked. She saw him, and he watched her every school day. But they didn't speak to each other until one day when Pat was struggling with some brown paper sacks of shopping and Alessandro offered to help her home.

The romance began, her first true love, her first lover. She spent every moment she could with Alessandro: he filled her days, her thoughts and her life. It was that unbearable first love, the one that catches your breath, that's so intense, so overflowing with energy, it's a surprise you don't explode.

They talked in Italian all the time; Pat had learned her lessons. They spent days off and holidays travelling around to Rome, Naples, and most often to nearby Lake Como where they would picnic by the water and he would whisper her name and they'd make love.

When the Omodie family said they were leaving Milan she didn't go with them but searched desperately for a job close to her man, near Alessandro's barber's. She rejected nanny and au pair positions all over the city until one location worked for her. The kids were a nightmare but that wasn't going to ruin her dream. Alessandro, a young twenty-three years old, was going to do that all by himself.

They were on one of their regular Sunday afternoon trips out to the Lakes. Alessandro was quiet and thoughtful as he laid out their blankets. They'd been together for more than a year and Pat thought he might be going to propose to her.

Instead, she shivered in the sun as he said:'Patti, I love you, but I can't ever marry you. My family have arranged for me to marry someone else. I have no choice, no choice at all.'

Pat couldn't believe it. It was absurd. Alessandro was from southern Italy, where the culture could be as strict as Islam, but an arranged marriage? In April 1969? She couldn't, couldn't understand.

Alessandro tried to explain how serious it was. His parents had discovered he was seeing an English girl. His father was so indignant he took a knife to his son's throat and hissed, 'You stay with this English girl over my dead body.'

Alessandro said they had to end their affair then and there. It was over, for ever.

'I'm so sorry, Patti, but there is no other way. I have no control over it. I have to do what my father is asking me.'

She begged him to change his mind. He could run back to England with her. They could hide in Italy. Go to France. America. It did no good. They were both crying as Alessandro drove them back to Milan. He gave her one final kiss when he dropped her off. It felt cold.

Pat sobbed and sobbed for weeks. She only slept when she was utterly worn out with exhaustion because her mind was spinning, asking questions around the clock. It was really just one question: why?

The only thing keeping her sane was the hope that it was all a mistake: Alessandro would come back to her, the

9

arranged wedding would be abandoned and all would be well.

That was a fantasy; the reality meant more heartache. Friends told her Alessandro had met his future wife and the wedding date had been set. She snapped. The crying stopped. With no more tears left in her, she went to see Alessandro at his barber's shop. Hysterical, she screamed for her lover to come out.

'You'll get me killed, Patti!' Alessandro shouted back. 'You'll get me killed if you do this! Go away before someone sees us.'

He slammed the door in Pat's face. With a loud crack he threw back the heavy bolt. It went into her heart.

She found the tears again. They flooded out as she limped off down the street. She was sobbing so much she could hardly see the two young guys asking if she was OK, if she wanted a lift home.

Love had turned into frustrated anger and Alessandro, the man she wanted so terribly, was the only one she could take it out on; cursing him, she was thinking in a mixture of English and Italian: 'Right! I'll show him what's what. *Vivi il presente.*'

Without a thought about what she was doing, she got into the back of what she soon realised was a very smart car. It seemed brand new. She could smell the leather.

The driver, who introduced himself as Luca, said: 'Momento!' They had to wait for another friend, just a couple of minutes and they would be on their way. They would look after her, take her home. She mustn't worry, must stop crying. The other guy, Franco, got in the back of the car with her.

Pat didn't care as the moments ticked on. She sat silently all wrapped up in her aching upset. It was the end of her world, of her life. She was traumatised. She felt dead inside.

Suddenly, the driver was talking to someone. There was a clunk and a pull at the front passenger door. A short, wiry young man with a flowing flop of black hair climbed in beside the driver.

He twisted, whirled around, and stared at Pat with a naughty grin: '*Ciao, bella! Ciao, tesora.*' ['Hi, lovely! Hi, beautiful!]

His name was Emilio. Emilio Di Giovine.

CHAPTER TWO
WONDERLAND

'To be honest, as this world goes,
is to be one man picked out of ten thousand.'

WILLIAM SHAKESPEARE,

HAMLET

Luca, the driver, invited Pat to a nightclub and she agreed. She wanted to forget Alessandro. She put on a yellow dress to brighten her spirits and went out intending to have some harmless fun.

That evening Luca's best pal Emilio Di Giovine once again magically materialised in his tight shirt and tighter pants. He arrived late at the noisy, smoke-filled nightclub, explaining that he'd crashed a borrowed car and the owner was not amused. Emilio was not bothered. As his friends jabbered questions about the accident, he shrugged: 'It happens.'

His eyes were watching Pat dancing and he was soon making his way across the crowded dance floor to talk to her. It was as if Luca didn't exist.

'Do you want me to take you home? Why don't you go out with me?' He said he would take her out the following night.

'You'd better not take me home,' she said. 'I came here with Luca.'

But Emilio came round the next night and the two of them went to a funfair. From then on, he kept coming to pick her up, each time driving a different car. They were all spanking new and when she queried this he told her: 'My dad has a garage.'

After stealing a kiss on an early date he said, 'Pat, you're the kind of girl I want to marry.'

Mum was twenty-three years old and she'd heard plenty of chat-up lines so she laughingly brushed this off as nonsense. It was silly, Italian Romeo talk from a boy who was only nineteen years old. Her instinct was to tell him to hop it. Yet it was nice to hear the passionate patter after the heartbreak of Alessandro. It was good for her self-esteem to feel wanted.

And so was his lifestyle. She couldn't get her head round the new cars: a Porsche on Tuesday, a Mercedes on Thursday and a nippy Alfa Romeo for Saturday and Sunday. There was always something new for the weekend.

'Emilio, what *do* you *do*?'

With a charismatic smile and not a hint of shame, he replied, 'I race cars and work as a mechanic at my father's garage.'

As far as Pat was concerned, he might have said he was going to the Moon along with Neil Armstrong and Buzz Aldrin who'd just become the first men to take a stroll up there. It didn't make sense to her. It was curiouser and curiouser. Their trips around town only confused her more. The flash cars weren't the attraction. He was like a magnet for people, who hurried over to talk to him as if they just wanted to be seen near him.

Everywhere he went his language was cash but in many bars and restaurants his money was foreign to them; the owners wouldn't take it, saying their meals and drinks were on the house. He wore bespoke suits, his shirts and ties from the Via Montenapoleone designer shops, his shoes imported, English and cap-toed. He was groomed to perfection, having a wet shave and his moustache trimmed every day at the barber's. There, his double espresso and his toasted cheese *panini* were always waiting as he took the central chair, like a celebrity. It was fascinating. She seemed to have stepped into some extraordinary wonderland.

And Emilio was a get-things-done kind of guy. Certainly, when Pat had problems with the family she was working for he was quick to sort things out.

One night after she put the kids to bed, the father tried to get it on with her. Pat realised he was horribly drunk and told him to get lost. She went off to bed in the room where she slept next to his daughter. She woke up with the guy trying to feel her up under the duvet and that was that. She ran out of the house and called Emilio.

'Pack your stuff,' he told her. 'You're not staying there. What's he going to do next?'

She went back to get her things but the family wouldn't open the door to her. When Emilio arrived Pat was a wreck, sobbing outside the apartment building. He took one look and told her to wait in his car. She tried to say he shouldn't do anything but he took off in a rush of virility.

Within minutes he'd returned with her bags all neatly packed. He'd 'sorted' the problem. The sex pest would never bother her again. She never found out what he had said – or done. Emilio had no difficulty finding a girlfriend who would let Pat stay until she found another job. By then they had become very much a couple and Pat found out she was pregnant with me.

They'd been lovers for just sixteen days.

Emilio was delighted and his parents were even more so at the prospect of their first grandchild. Emilio was the adored eldest son and Nan opened the doors of her home to him and Pat.

At that time, Nan's had two bedrooms, a huge front room, kitchen and bathroom, and eleven kids, aged from nineteen downwards, with Auntie Angela only a few weeks more than a twinkle in Grandpa's eye. Mum and Dad were given their own bedroom. Nan and Grandpa had the other. The rest had to lump it where they could. It was pandemonium. There were kids everywhere, crying, shouting, screaming, laughing, and they all seemed to be fighting. It was like a coven of hysterical little demons.

'They're all mad here,' thought Pat with a grim grin to herself.

It was all falling into place, as if her destiny was mapped out for her. She had no choice. She wasn't really in love with Emilio. She was still in love with Alessandro and Emilio was her boyfriend on the rebound. He helped her.

When she was a few weeks' pregnant she went to Blackpool and told her parents, who were distraught. Where was the man who'd got their girl pregnant? Where was this Emilio? They were horrified, in their quiet, behind-the-curtains English way, at how things had turned out. They had hoped Pat would return quickly after her Italian adventure but she had arrived home to announce she was pregnant and was going back for good to raise their first grandchild. Their big, repeated question was: 'Who is this Emilio?'

Pat didn't tell them because she still wasn't sure herself. Instead she offered: 'He's a good man. He's looking after me. I'm happy.'

And deep down Pat really hoped she would be.

When she returned to Piazza Prealpi, she started getting affectionate with his parents, with all the brothers and sisters, learning much if not all about the family's history. Her emotions were all over the place, but she wanted to belong, to make it work with the young Emilio and the baby that was on the way. She'd never met a man quite like him before.

'Better,' he'd always say, 'to live like a lion for one day than live like a sheep for one hundred years.'

Yet even in the Mafia, there were questions of propriety. Nan put pressure on Emilio to 'do the right thing'.

Only eighteen days after I was born, on 9 March 1970, they became man and wife at a registry office close to Piazza Prealpi, with Emilio in a dark suit and Pat in an understated brown dress she'd bought at C&A in Blackpool. Grandpa Rosario, who was a witness, looked as if he was at a funeral. Pat's parents weren't there. The wedding reception was pasta at Nan's.

There, Pat overheard her husband and father-in-law talking in the kitchen.

'Emilio, I'm worried about this girl. She's going to ask too many questions. She's English – she won't understand how things work. She could really fuck things up for us.'

Grandpa was told there was no problem. No one was going to stand in the family's way, certainly not Pat. It was business as usual.

As if to prove it, Emilio celebrated his wedding night by going out drinking and gambling with his smuggling crews. His bride spent the night alone, looking after the new baby – me – and worrying about our future.

Emilio was nimble-witted, nerveless and remarkably fluent in violence and villainy. He was an heir to that audacity. Just like his mother.

Nan was born on 14 November 1931 in San Sperato, right by the tip of Calabria, on the Strait of Messina across from Mount Etna in Sicily, as deep in the wilds as you can go. Her family were partisans in the mountains during the Second World War, and 'partisan' in their world meant they were fighting for each other, for themselves.

They were infamous. They fought fiercely against the Germans, against Mussolini. They were against anybody and everybody. They quite liked the American soldiers for the black market in chocolate. In their own interests, they dealt in protection, extortion and contraband. It was more ruthless than sophisticated.

They were traditionalists, keeping the faiths of the 'Ndrangheta, whose bad business goes back to Italian unification in 1861. The 'Ndrangheta didn't need secret codes because the Calabrian dialect is impenetrable. In the early days the poor but proud and angry Calabrians banded together against the rich squires who'd taken over what they saw as their land. There were about 400 people in San Sperato and most families managed to grab a chunk of land.

It hadn't changed much when Nan was growing up with eleven brothers and sisters, a family bred to war in the Calabrian hills. All of them were crushed into a half-built two-bedroom stone house. The Serraino family, like the others, grew olives and lemons, but they also dealt in contraband cigarettes and liquor, mostly cognac stolen from Calabria's huge Gioia Tauro port – Italy's 'passport to the world' – which was under 'Ndrangheta control. In the shade of melon stalls on the dirt roads all around the countryside, the illicit booze and tobacco were bought and sold. The police collected their payoffs in kind, bottles of brandy and wine, a couple of cartons of smokes, towards the end of Friday afternoons.

'Have a nice weekend,' they were told.

It was the family legacy, the family economics, venal but effective: control the trade, supply the demand, and fear no one. Indeed, keep the authorities close to you, pay them off, corrupt or kill them. The Mafia code: keep your friends close, your enemies closer. Perfection would be everybody on the payroll.

It didn't always work. Some of the police, not many, were straight, or under some sort of regional government control and obliged to make the occasional arrest. That meant that many of those around San Sperato – for everyone had some connection with the 'black' economy – spent at least a short time in jail.

That included my great-grandfather Domenico 'Mico' Serraino, who was given six months in Calabria Prison for a robbery in the summer of 1947. They didn't take into consideration any of his other fifty or so offences – that year – as somehow they were never registered in the paperwork.

Domenico Serraino was known as 'The Fox', and was cunning in the extreme. His wife, my great-grandma Margherita Medora, was from a similar family. They were peasants who hadn't had any schooling. He lived in a narrow world: sons of sons were on pedestals, sons of daughters were undeserving of his attention. The sons of sons were gods but grandchildren with a different surname were not allowed to eat with him. If they came close he would chase them away with the back of his hand. Nan was a blessed Serraino.

It was her job to visit her father Mico in prison, to take provisions, cigarettes and wine. The prison guards would receive their 'allowance' during the visit. She was very much a sweet sixteen-year-old in appearance but already wily in the way of a born Calabrian, truly The Fox's daughter. That gave her the confidence to take a chance on romance with the fresh-faced twenty-year-old prison guard who chatted her up during her visits. There was a real sparkle between them. Rosario Di Giovine was new to the prison, new to the area, but linked by bloodline to the South. His dad worked in Rome in the prison service. It was just after the war and work was hard to find so his dad got him this state job. It most certainly wasn't a vocation.

Still, he didn't realise that getting involved with Maria Serraino could get him killed. Just for spinning her a line.

There was no way Nan could take a prison guard home to meet the family. It would be like bringing home the cops. She'd have been disowned and Grandpa would certainly have fallen off a cliff.

Nan found a way. She offered to do the washing for the prison guards in return for a little money. It was an excuse to keep visiting the prison after her father was freed. And Rosario Di Giovine was a quick learner in the ways of Calabria. They kept their affair secret and later my grandpa quietly left the prison service and avoided the cafés and bars the other officers went to. His time there didn't even stay on his CV. It was as if it had never been. Instead, he became a truck driver, a very useful skill in the Serraino family.

Rosario had a way with him but his charm was tested as Nan's father and brothers watched closely. In those days you weren't ever left alone with a man. You had to have an escort. If you went out for an ice cream you had to have a chaperone. That's how it worked. And it worked double for newcomers like Grandpa. He could feel the eyes on him. But true love always …

As a young couple time dragged for them, so before long they'd run off together to another village in the mountains. The family realised what had been going on and, sure enough, Nan was pregnant.

The atmosphere was difficult, with tension and violent arguments between Grandpa and Nan's brothers, but circumstances dominated everything. They married and my dad, Emilio, was born twenty days before Christmas in 1949. The Serraino–Di Giovine dynasty had begun and so had the baby production line. While Grandpa became a trusted lieutenant and started driving contraband for the family, Nan began giving birth.

In those tough post-war years, even with all the ducking and diving, the thieving and smuggling, it was an almighty struggle to stay ahead. The ways of Calabria were always respected. My nan was the one who kept everything together and she was always taking in strays, both kids and dogs. She was a lovely, genuinely giving woman, but she had a ruthless streak in her. If you did something bad to her family or disrespected them, she wouldn't think twice about getting you beaten to a pulp. Just like that she would kick off. That was the world she had always lived in.

When her son Emilio was four years old his grandfather made him watch a pig being slaughtered. The pig's throat was slit in front of him and the blood dripped into a bucket. This little boy had to immerse his arm up to the elbow in the blood and stir it so it wouldn't coagulate. There wasn't room for waste because they wanted to make a batch of blood sausage. Emilio had to keep stirring the blood. That was the side of the family that made him a man. That's how all the children, the masculine children, as they put it, were brought up.

Kindness to strays and buckets of blood? One extreme to the other.

By 1963, Emilio had six brothers and four sisters and they were all living like chickens, constantly scratching for space and food. It was then Nan decided life would be better in Milan. It was like moving abroad, going to Australia. It was faraway and foreign to them. But Nan packed her bags and her kids and moved north. She had some money saved, and she had guile and single-minded determination. It was enough to get them an apartment on the Piazza Prealpi, which is where *La Signora* launched her criminal organisation (which was worthy of that title from the start).

She made associations within the Milanese underworld but most important was the established Calabrian connection: from there, at first, came the cigarettes and booze, the currency of her start-up operation. Her gang were a young, wild bunch. Over time all her kids were in the act: Emilio and his tough-guy brothers Domenico, Antonio, Franco, Alessandro, Filippo and Guglielmo. And his sisters, Rita, Mariella, Domenica and Natalina had walk-on parts too. And the 'strays' were thankful to help by running errands.

Nan was ever-purposeful; nothing was done by chance. She spoke with a distinct and difficult dialect. It's very hard to understand – she really needs subtitles – unless you've grown up with it. However, her meaning was always crystal clear.

The Piazza Prealpi, fifteen minutes from central Milan on a slow traffic day, was pivotal to her empire. The square housed an assortment of market stalls with flapping awnings and flaking paint where you could buy the fresh basics for breakfast, lunch and dinner. On other smaller but busier open-air stalls there were younger, louder guys selling newspapers, magazines, booze and cigarettes. It was a downbeat neighbourhood of city life and lives. But families didn't have to go any further for their needs. The cafés, bars and restaurants were open from dawn until the small hours. There were always people about, happier to sit outside than in the squashed, dull blocks of council flats which comprise the Piazza. There was an eager, waiting market for anyone with commercial enterprise, a bit of get up and go.

Nan instantly realised the potential to sell cheap cigarettes and hooky alcohol in the square and make a fortune. She knew that contraband bought in volume and without duty could be sourced and sold much cheaper than it was at present, but still at immense profit.

She didn't rush at it. She began slowly by selling to the shopkeepers at knockdown prices which became lower and lower, so low that people came from all over the city to buy. She met the demand.

Nan held 'board' meetings every morning in her kitchen. Once her children reached a useful age they were told what to steal, how to steal it and who to move it to. Go here. Get this. Do that. Speak to him. Come back to me. If one child ratted on another, told their mother that one of the others had stolen something, the telltale was beaten. Mercilessly. The rule was you said nothing, you kept quiet or the punishment was harsh. The code of silence, *omertà,* trumped blood bonds. Nan's law was: 'You have to shut up.'

Emilio and the others never went to school. Nan was the headmistress, discipline was the whack of a big, stained wooden soup spoon. There was one supreme teaching: 'First make them fear you. Then they will respect you.'

Nan had few dreads. Maybe God, the Catholic church. I would watch her in the afternoons when she stepped outside the apartment and put her chair out on the street. She would sit there quietly holding her rosary beads and I'd get goose bumps hearing her prayer: 'God, forgive me for anything I've done today.'

Yet, the legend was she knew things before God did. She had eyes in the back of God's head. She certainly paid him off. The Church was the only place her money went, other than the family and professional expenses. She gave thousands to the Church, perhaps to assuage her guilt. Maybe it was bribery of the Almighty – paying for a place in Heaven? She used to send fabulous clothes (stolen, of course) inside the prisons. She gave thieves heroin: it was a vicious circle. She donated all kinds of goodies to the nuns and priests who worked with the poor in Milan. No one ever asked where they came from, which was just as well. I think it made her feel a bit better inside, that she was balancing things out. None of the family went to confession because everybody thought the priest would have to be paid off to keep his mouth shut. I'm not sure if Nan was bartering with God but she certainly did that with every living thing.

Elsewhere it was cut-throat business. She abruptly axed the legitimate suppliers who had been dealing to the Piazza Prealpi stallholders for decades. It was simple business from both sides of the market stalls. Nan could sell *everything* cheaper and eventually almost all the shopkeepers and land-lords in the Piazza took daily deliveries of knockdown stock.

Supposedly, Grandpa Rosario worked as a regular truck driver. It was a pretty transparent 'cover' to prove the family had legitimate income. All that was regular were his trips – over the border to Switzerland where cut-price cigarettes were available.

He and Emilio ran the smuggling syndicate. Emilio was only fifteen years old when he began running a team of two dozen teenage drivers to and from Switzerland with secret compartments under the back seats of their Fiat 500s jammed with contraband cartons. In this way, more than ten thousand packs of cigarettes a day were delivered to Nan's. When they arrived, crow bars were used to wrench forward the back seats to reveal where the cartons were concealed.

The other legitimate suppliers were severely pissed off. They complained to the police. Uniformed officers felt obliged to investigate and they became regular visitors, always leaving with one or two twenty-pack boxes of Marl-boros and a kiss on each cheek from Nan. As word got around the precincts the police faces changed and the gifts became more lavish: expensive jewellery, champagne, a stereo system. She could afford the tempting payoffs.

Nan's ability to obtain cheap cigarettes and move them on without fuss or interference from the police earned her a reputation across Milan. Soon she became a major fence dealing in all manner of stolen merchandise, whether it was a car radio or a gold Rolex, a cashmere sweater or a used video. If anybody nicked anything anywhere it would go to my Nan's first. She had first refusal. When someone brought a stolen goat she didn't blink; she tethered it, fattened it and sold it ten days later. There was nothing Nan wouldn't buy and nothing she couldn't sell on at a profit.

And she wanted no competition. If any opposition tried to move in, she dealt with it the Calabrian way. She eradicated the problem. She carved out, literally in some cases, a fearsome reputation. With the police in their pocket it was made very obvious the Di Giovines were the kingpins. The family was devious in many things.Nan hadn't been educated and couldn't read or write but she could count money. Very well and very quickly. Nan was the Godmother. People would come to her with their problems and she would help. It established loyalty and connections.

She ran her organisation with military precision and controlled it by military methods. The rules and the consequences for breaking or challenging them were severe. If someone had to be punished Emilio would be instructed, given the assignment. If he was pulling the trigger to whack someone on the street at 11 p.m., it was Nan who had told him where to aim the gun five minutes earlier.

And there was always a beef to sort out. If a rival came into the Piazza trying to deal stolen goods or sell smuggled cigarettes, Emilio would go to sort it. The square belonged to the Di Giovines and my nan's view was that the bastards had to know who was the boss. Emilio was the Enforcer, dealing out beatings, kicking people to the brink of death. He was short, only 5 foot 4 inches tall, because he'd had a milk allergy as a baby. They fed him tomatoes instead, and the doctors said the lack of calcium stunted his growth. But despite his short stature, no one doubted how deadly he was. He had a reputation for being big down there, well proportioned. His family nickname was *Canna Lunga*, the long cane. His brothers used to joke about it. He was very good-looking, very charismatic. He just had a way.

When he was younger Emilio wore insteps in his shoes to make him taller. But it was confidence that gave him his swagger on the streets; a brash Napoleon, he did not fear anyone. Idiots would always get one warning to clear out the area but the second time they would get hit.

'Fuck up a third time and I'll kill you.' He meant it.

He got results and his fearless determination to protect and control the area for the family attracted businessmen, shopkeepers and families with their own difficulties. They would go to Nan's, leave cash and wait for Emilio to solve their problems. With that, the family had one of the most profitable protection rackets in Milan. And if protection duties were slow there was also the flip side, extortion.

'Maria, these guys keep coming in and stealing stuff off my shelves.'

'La Signora, some fellas smashed up my bar on Sunday night.'

'Maria, this guy two blocks down is setting his prices so low I am going to go bust and I can't buy from you any more.'

'Send for Emilio' was the chorus, the solution; going to see Nan meant things were dealt with more efficiently and far quicker than if they went to the police – who Nan was paying to keep their noses out anyway. She had all the ends covered in her kingdom. For Nan this was a gold mine.

However, it meant that my kindergarten was an armed compound and my criminal career began when I was a few months old. That's when I went on my first smuggling mission. The police have the photographs to prove it.

CHAPTER THREE
MARLBORO WOMAN

'I said blow the bloody doors off!'

MICHAEL CAINE AS CHARLIE CROKER,

THE ITALIAN JOB, 1969

When my mum first moved into the Piazza Prealpi apartment it had been customised for crime. Nan was an exceptionable presence in Milan and despite the payoffs police raids were always a threat. There were compartments, nothing more than holes in the wall riddled around behind the kitchen skirting boards, where Nan kept handguns. There were other hiding places – beneath radiators, in cisterns, at the neighbours' – for more guns and cash. Many of them were places where only a small child's arm could reach. She was a female Fagin, my nan.

And her den, the apartment, was a constant bustle. Everyone was asking for more – more tobacco, more bottles of booze, more anything-off-the-back-of-a-lorry, and, always, always, more money.

Mum was dazed by the chaotic and crazed lifestyle; there were usually so many people sleeping over she couldn't count the number. Names? She was still keeping up with the names of Dad's brothers and sisters. So from dawn till midnight she just nodded hello when the scores of strangers marched into the apartment carrying boxes. Mum had an idea of what was going on around her but never imagined the scale of it; any questions never quite got an answer. She didn't push my grandparents; she was grateful for all they were doing for her and for me.

In return for the generosity, Mum helped run the household, working with Nan and Dad's sisters cleaning, washing, ironing and preparing food. There was always someone around to watch me, play with me. I had all the love and attention in the world.

Mum learned to bake bread, make pasta and create authentic Italian meals, mostly using recipes by Ada Boni, the famous 1950s Italian cookery author. She favoured feed-everybody dishes like Chicken Tetrazzini, a casserole with chicken and spaghetti in a creamy cheese sauce. Nan would be up at six in the morning cooking. In between doing her deals, she was at the stove. We'd wake up to the smell of food. It wouldn't just be sauces; she would cook all sorts of dishes, including veal, chicken, fish, even tripe. She had a freezer full of meat, polythene bags stuffed with cash hidden among the ice cubes, and boxes and boxes of nicked gear in her larders. She was a regular Delia Smith, but with a .38 revolver in the spice cupboard and a couple of other handguns in the dried pasta. Instead of shopping lists, she would have notebook catalogues of dubious contacts for every possible chore, surrounded by cans of chopped tomatoes. Cooking was her therapy. She never went out. She never did anything. She didn't smoke, she didn't drink. Her interests were totally family and business, the Calabrian way. And I adored her. She always had time for me no matter what dramas were going on – and being an Italian household everybody knew about them. You heard them! Very loudly. But even the noise was a comfort to me. It meant that the family were all around and I was safe. It was my warm blanket.

Nan would cook lunch for whoever was there and Mum would be in charge of supper, when there were always at least twenty to feed. Mum felt she was beginning to belong. Her spoken Italian was good but bastardised, using the family dialect, a magicking of Calabrian and Sicilian; she so enchanted the market stallholders when she was out shopping that they called her 'the blonde Sicilian'.

But she was aware she wasn't having the same effect on Dad. She'd prayed she would feel the same heart-stopping emotions she had felt for Alessandro. That it would work out between her and Dad. That he would grow out of being a jack-the-lad driven by his lust for new excitement, for girls and fast cars. What she didn't and couldn't fully understand at first is what it truly meant to have the blood of the Serraino–Di Giovine family surging through him.

Her education didn't take too long. There was little to do most evenings, after the cooking and the washing up, but talk. And, more importantly, listen. She never heard the words Mafia or 'Ndrangheta for they were never spoken. She realised there was a lot of ducking and diving going on, but if Emilio was making money dealing in dodgy cigarettes it didn't seem too serious to her. On the crime scale she thought it was a bit like bringing in too much duty free.

Certainly, that's how the family's ever-growing mass smuggling operation was presented to her. And Mum heard what she wanted to hear. She was wise to do that for she was about to be recruited by the 'Ndrangheta.

Dad's smuggling crews criss-crossing in and out of Switzerland at the Italian border town of Lago di Lugano were being increasingly hassled at the checkpoints. He decided to 'disguise' the trips as sightseeing and romantic days out and sent drivers across accompanied by women. Dad began taking Mum on his own runs. It worked: the police pressure eased, and the volume of cigarettes being brought back to Nan's doubled within a few weeks.

Dad tried not to let Mum in on the extent of the family operations. It was a feeble effort. She saw him carrying a gun. She saw the police arrive threateningly and leave happy. If she did question any of the bewildering events the answer was always: 'There's no need to worry or get involved, so don't.'

Her big question – to herself – was when our family was going to get its own home. So, in her protective way, she was just happy Emilio was out earning some money, which she hoped would bankroll an escape from the shoebox life at Nan's. That we would be a family unit, not part of a daily and increasingly crazy cavalcade at Nan's. She wanted to raise me in Italy where she had made friends.

Vital to that dream of domestic bliss was her relationship with Dad. She couldn't ignore her inner self which told her she didn't truly love him; they were brought together by circumstances. Yet falling pregnant was a big deal and, rebound guy or no rebound guy, the rules were you stayed together and tried to make it work. Well, that was how she saw it.

After the long kitchen table drama when I was born and she held me in her arms, her emotions, her heart and mothering instincts, took over. Her life purpose was now to care for me and she didn't want to do it as a single mum. She wanted me to have a mum and dad.

For Dad, his only concern then was business, which was booming and expanding into even more dangerous territory. The Turkish gangs running drugs throughout Milan were hiring 'money collectors', teams of hard men to bring in the payments. Dad started making tidy sums from this but saw the dealers themselves getting lavish payoffs of more than £10,000 a time, which was enticing. He was still indulging in his favourite pastimes, stealing cars and dating girls. When the girls met him he always had a polished Porsche, a red Ferrari – he likes red – or a new Alfa Romeo. A racing driver? It didn't look or sound to the girls like the buckets of bullshit it really was.

Mum was just keeping her head above it all. Dad was gone a lot of the time and she was pretty sure he was having affairs but she couldn't prove it. She was lucky to be single-minded and determined, for the toll on her was incessant; flirting with postnatal depression and not knowing what shocks or surprises would present themselves each day – and there were usually one or two – she remained strong.

Mum desperately wanted her own space, and Dad finally got us out of Nan's and into a small rented apartment. It wasn't grand but it was our home and an escape from the bedlam of Nan's house, where there was another baby, Auntie Angela, who was only a month older than me, and the raging testosterone in the house with all my uncles. They were growing up, doing their own thing, having their own bit of business here and there. There was fighting between them but nobody would dare fight with them. It was 'I hate you, but nobody else can hate you.' If any harm came to one of them, then everybody would band together. It was like a circus with lots of zany characters and hoops being jumped through. Nan was the ringmaster in a sauce-stained apron. Some people would shrink back when she shouted but I knew she only raised her voice to those she loved. If she shouted at you, everything was OK. Silence wasn't golden, not at all.

I was now very much part of it, by blood, and that's a lifetime bond. And because of me, so was Mum. But for much of the time it was the life of a single mum. She didn't know what Dad was doing, where he was going or who he was seeing from one day to the next. He was all over the place with his smugglers. The consignments grew and grew. But the bigger they were, the bigger the problem of moving them into the country.

Mum had been to England to show me off to her parents and returned with a present, an elaborate carrycot with lots of side pockets for nappies and all the other baby paraphernalia. When Dad examined it, he noticed there was also a slot underneath where he could hide dozens of cartons of cigarettes. Instead of a traditional family lunch, he began taking us out in the grey Fiat 500 for a 45-minute drive to Lake Como, where we would collect the cigarettes and then return for tea with some of the contraband concealed in the car and me lying in my cot on the rest of it. Dad was so pleased with this scheme, he took photographs of me lying on a Marlboro mattress. There's one picture where I have a cigarette on my lips, the Marlboro baby. Little did he know that the police would come upon these pictures one day in the future.

Mum and Dad's life appeared to settle, but there's no smoke without fire. He was still vanishing without warning and leaving no message telling where he was. Business. Always business. But he was around enough for Mum to get pregnant again. An accident. And a tragic one in so many ways.

Dad continued fooling around. He was still only twenty-one years old when he got involved with a blonde English dancer called Melanie Taylor, who was touring with a cabaret show. She thought she was in love with him. She was only one of the girls he'd been seeing but it had been going on for some time. Mum, heavily pregnant, heard his brothers talking about the relationship. Finally, she lost it. She marched off to the bar where the dancing girls went in the evening. She burst in, telling them to let this slag Melanie know that the guy she was screwing was her husband and she was expecting another baby with him.

When word got back to Dad about what had happened, he calmly walked into the bar and told Melanie and her friends that Mum was mad. He was cold and calculating and claimed she was pregnant by someone else and he was leaving her over it. Everyone believed what they wanted to believe.

Mum had vented much of the rage from her system, and she was mentally and physically tired and weary of it all, so she got on with having her second baby. She knew it was going to be another little girl. Dad didn't bother to turn up for the birth, which this time, at Mum's insistence, was at the local hospital. My sister Rosella was born but it was two days later before Dad visited and even then he turned up with another woman.

Nan saw red at this and dragged the girl, who didn't know any better, out of the car and battered her, shouting: 'You ugly whore!' She loved my dad, but she didn't like what he was doing, so she took it out on the nearest person who wasn't family.

When Dad got to the bedside my mum said: 'You've just been with other women, haven't you?'

'I swear on this baby's life I haven't.'

It was terrible, tragic. Tiny Rosella died three weeks later. She'd had lots of health complications but officially her death was down to tetanus.

Mum was devastated. She felt lost, and she knew that was definitely it with my dad. It was over. I was a little more than a year old. Mum had one baby and no income. She couldn't afford to keep paying the rent at the apartment, so she had nowhere to stay.

She went 'home' – in other words, she went to Nan's. That's all that made sense to her. Nan was on Mum's side. Family.

And, of course, business. Nan paid for Mum to have driving lessons. When she had her licence – Nan didn't want any traffic laws being broken – she started in the cold mists of winter doing solo cigarette runs. She'd drive to Lake Como and also into Switzerland when cheaper consignments were on offer. Sometimes one of my uncles would go along.

It was her way of displaying loyalty to the family and earning some money for them. All the time I was happily being looked after by Nan and her troops of helpers. Dad? He was going up in the underworld, his enterprises far more dangerous and lucrative than before. His lifestyle reflected that.

For Mum it was make do as she could. She wanted us to get our own place away from the crowded craziness of Nan's and put us down for council accommodation. It didn't take long. I was nearly three years old when we moved into Quarto Oggiaro, into the 'Mussolini flats', the largest social housing district of Milan. The concrete camp of a neighbourhood started by the Italian dictator was home to immigrants, first from southern Italy and, when we moved in, from Turkey and Yugoslavia, making it a colourful melting pot.

For Mum it was our first home together and special to her. But not to anyone else. It's the roughest place in Milan, and

Milan's a big city; a poor, grey downtrodden estate for thousands of poor people, chilled in the city fogs of winter, oppressive in the summer heat.

We had a big room, twenty by twenty, that we slept in, ate in, did everything in. It was token rent, the equivalent of a couple of pounds a week. We didn't get much for that: one bed for the two of us, a small kitchen corridor and a little toilet. We didn't have a bath or a shower. We'd go to Nan's house to have a really decent wash. If not, we used to have to go to the public showers. I'd grip Mum's hand as we stood in line to take our turn under the water. It didn't matter what time or what day we were there, the water was always freezing cold: almost refreshing in the summer but cruel in winter.

It was about a fifteen-minute ride on the number 7 or number 12 tram and then a ten-minute walk from the Quarto Oggiaro over to Nan's where I still saw my dad. He was always smiling when he saw me and I loved it. I wanted to hug him for ever. Yet, in a little kid way, I couldn't understand why I didn't see him every day. Didn't he love me as much as I loved him?

He wouldn't be seen dead at our place, the poorest area in the city. He drove a chocolate-coloured Porsche – this one was paid for – and lived in a really exclusive area. 'Why are we like this, and my dad has got all that?' I wondered.

He took me to meet Daniella, one of his girlfriends, who had a son about my age. We went to a toyshop and he told us to choose something. I was used to having the cheapest things and picked a little dressing table with make-up and hairbrushes. The lad picked a powered pedal car that you sat in – it would have cost a fortune. I liked my dressing table but later the family teased me that the lad's present was much better than mine and I got fed up with my dad about that.

Mum was the star. She worked all hours at the Upim market, which sold everything, a sort of mini Tesco. She did shifts to work around my school timetable.

I didn't speak English, only Italian. I understood 'sit down' and 'thank you' but Mum only spoke Italian to me. She wanted me to *belong*. We had picture books, *Pinocchio*, *Alice in Wonderland* and other kids' stories. The teachers made you eat courgettes and go to sleep in the afternoon and I hated all of that. They'd prop up cot beds and we had to lie there for about forty-five minutes and have a little sleep. I pretended I was asleep because you'd get told off if you moved or said a word.

We had white overalls and each class had its own different-coloured little collar – mine was red and orange. The overalls would be various shades and sizes, some better, some worse, depending on where you bought them, but you had to have them on top of your normal clothes. It was like any school uniform, an attempt to stop there being any 'them' and 'us' in the class or playground. Most of the kids were deprived anyway for it was that sort of neighbourhood, and on the stifling hot days of summer that left you breathless it could smell like a bad Spanish holiday.

For Carnival Day on 17 February I always had to borrow an outfit from Auntie Angela. She got the costume and I had to borrow it. Whatever she had, I wouldn't get a choice. I was a fairy one time when I was very little. One year I got a Spanish flamenco costume that Angela had never worn and I was very happy; that was special.

The school was a five-minute walk from home and Mum would drop me off just before 8 a.m. when lessons and her Upim shift began. It was all co-ordinated. I finished school at 1.30 p.m., just as Mum's first shift ended, so she picked me up and we'd go to Nan's, then she went back to work until 7 p.m. Nobody from school ever came back to my nan's. Mum kept that part of our life separate. Classmates would visit at Mum's. Her friend Linda's daughter Simona was in my class and her son Luca was a little younger. I played ball and rode my bike with them and a lot of other kids in the yard at the Mussolini flats.

I also caught nits, one of the neighbourhood hazards. I heard Mum saying, 'Marisa, you're not going to like this but I've no choice,' and the next thing huge clumps of hair, my long, curly ringlets, were falling to the ground. When I looked in the mirror a little boy was staring back at me. I stood there screaming with tears rolling down my face. I was wearing red wellies, a red top and jeans and a shaven head. Mum took one of her 'arty' photographs.

That was a big drama for me. As a youngster I was protected from all the other dramas that were going on around me. Nan's was always warm and comfortable when

I stayed there in the afternoons and early evenings. There were more people and more room than at our place, and I loved my nan's food. Meals seemed to last for hours. I had my cousins to play with and the family would never, ever leave us out in any way. It was 'my house is your house'. When I went there it felt like my home. As soon as Mum and I walked through the door Nan stopped whatever she was doing and walked across the room and scooped me up in her huge arms. As she wrapped me up, pulled me close and kissed me on the end of my nose, I felt as though no one could hurt me. In her arms I would never come to any harm. She was always very giving and cuddly. I thought it was an amazing place. I'd never seen so many people in one house at the same time. It was full of excitement and love.

After meals I'd play with my skipping rope in the yard along with Auntie Angela, until it was too dark to see and we had to come inside. Then we'd chase the family dog, an Alsatian called Yago, all around the house until his barking became so loud that Grandpa would tell us to quit winding him up.

Everyone loved that animal but Grandpa. He hated it. One week when he had to travel to Calabria on family business he packed up his truck and hid Yago in the back. When he reached Calabria he turfed the dog out into the woods and drove off.

Nan was beside herself when he told her Yago had gone missing in Calabria. Then a miracle occurred. Three months later when Nan answered the door to a neighbour, in walked

Yago. Like everyone else, he had come back to my Nan. It turned out Grandpa hadn't taken him quite as far as he said he had, but Yago had still found his way home from right across the other side of Milan.

I used to sit next to Nan and put my head on her generous chest and she'd talk quietly and scratch my head. I would fall asleep to that and her voice. It was lovely. It felt comforting. I didn't know what she was thinking about. Or what she was plotting.

While I was at school, Nan and Dad were also getting lessons: about other ways to make money, including the Italian gangster growth industry – kidnapping. Huge worldwide headlines revolved around the abduction for ransom of John Paul Getty III. His father ran the Italian end of the family oil business from Rome and he'd grown up there. And that's where he was snatched in July 1973. The kidnappers from the 'Ndrangheta wanted 17 million US dollars for the sixteen-year-old's safe return.

The family, headed by John Paul Getty I, believed it was a hoax. The next ransom note was held up by a strike by Italian postal workers. The 'Ndrangheta decided to emphasise their seriousness. In November 1973 an envelope was delivered with a lock of hair, a human ear and a note saying: 'This is Paul's ear. If we don't get 3.2 million US dollars within ten days, then the other ear will arrive. In other words, he will arrive in little bits.'

Astonishingly, the boy's fabulously wealthy grandfather continued to negotiate. Finally, he paid 2.8 million US dollars and his grandson was found alive in southern Italy in December the same year. No one was ever arrested.

Everyone in my family took great interest in the case. Nan and Dad saw it as part of the Wild West that some areas of Italy were turning into. And an opportunity: not to get involved directly with their 'Ndrangheta brethren in the South, but to exploit the situation.

It was only a few years after the 'French Connection' – the huge operation that trafficked heroin from Marseilles to New York, which was turned into the 1971 Oscar-winning movie – and the stories of the profits involved remained legend. While the Italian authorities, politicians and *carabinieri* were focused on the plague of kidnapping, their attention and resources were taken away from drug trafficking, now the other booming business of the age. For Nan and Dad the mechanics were exactly like dealing in cigarettes. The big difference was the product. It was much, much more international and profitable, a multi-multi-million dollar industry.

And lethal for all involved.

CHAPTER FOUR
ROOM SERVICE

'We seek him here, we seek him there ...
Is he in Heaven? – Is he in Hell?
That demmed, elusive Pimpernel.'

BARONESS EMMUSKA ORCZY,
THE SCARLET PIMPERNEL, 1905

Dad was a captain of the new industries, a crime lord, and was acting and living like one. He was turning into a proper Godfather, with scores of soldiers under his command. He seemed to be everywhere but nowhere. He was always wanted by the police for something, even if it was just some petty crime. He was never in one place for long – he scowled out of many passport photographs. The family knew him as 'Gypsy' because he criss-crossed the borders of Europe and into Turkey and North Africa.

His power base was Milan. Companies, bars and restaurants were on the payroll, as well as, most importantly, the authorities. This was Nan's speciality, her business version of tender loving care – bullshit and cash, and lots of both. In pecking order she tied up the lawyers who brought in the magistrates who knew the right judges to approach and fix. She flicked through the corruption process like a pack of cards.

And Dad was just as quickly shuffling his affections. It was rare that he had Italian girlfriends. They arrived on his arm from all over the planet. Mum made sure she had good relationships with his girlfriends now, for she wanted me to stay close to him and she wanted to be comfortable with the girls if I was going to spend any time with them. It wasn't so difficult for Mum because she had never really loved Dad anyway. She just let go. She was never real friends with him; they tolerated each other because of me.

I got on with most of his girls. Melanie, whose father was a bigwig in the RAF, even took a comb to my nits, which is beyond the call of girlfriend duty. I stayed with her and Dad a few times. I loved the sleepovers and being close to my dad. Dad being there was the most important part of the visits. There was a subliminal feeling I could not experience with any other person. That father and daughter connection. It was different and exciting to be with him. Dad was always very affectionate. He'd mess around with me, we'd have fun. All his girls made a fuss of me, and I liked that.

There were lots of them but Effie the Paraguayan – Miss Paraguay – was special. She looked like a proper Inca woman and behaved almost like a man. She had one of those Aztec top haircuts, and she sat there at my Nan's smoking a cigar! The family all thought this was great.

Dad lived well. He moved into a luxurious apartment in Milano 2, a residential set-up in Segrate, a new town built by one of Silvio Berlusconi's companies. It was traffic-free, with bridges and walkways, a gym and a lake in the grounds. It was very upmarket and far removed from the lifestyle Mum and I had. But if Mum ever said anything about this, he retorted, 'My mother's looking after you, isn't she?'

Yet Dad didn't always get it all his way. He was seriously involved with a stunning French girl but she took a fancy to his sister, my Auntie Mariella. They used to come to my mum's to be together, to get it on. I came home from school one day to find them in the back of our blue Mini with the white roof. 'What are they doing?' I wondered. 'Why is my dad's girlfriend in there with my aunt?'

Much as Mum tried to keep it quiet and help, Dad found out and gave my Auntie Mariella a right kicking up the bum; he broke something on her spine, almost crippling her. He didn't do anything to his girlfriend. Family weren't meant to betray you.

I was puzzled about it in a little kid sort of way. I couldn't understand why everyone was upset. Mum told me not to say anything about seeing them together. She probably thought 'Up yours!' to my dad. I hope so. No one else would have dared do that.

Dad was doing whatever he wanted, whatever he felt like, but he was too much of a showman and Nan's payoffs couldn't guarantee one hundred per cent protection. In 1974 there was a sudden clean-out at City Hall and the appointment of a new police chief with his own set of magistrates. It takes a little time for corruption to seep through the system so, against the odds, a warrant was issued charging Emilio Di Giovine with handling stolen goods. The hunt, the game, was on.

Nan's apartment is in a courtyard block of about twenty homes. It's quite a walk from corner to corner. When the police came for my dad one day he thought he was being clever and stole quickly over to the opposite corner from Nan's. He walked straight into the cops.

They had no photograph of their suspect. They stopped him. Looked at him. Then asked: 'Do you know who Emilio Di Giovine is?'

'Oh yes, I've heard of him.'

'What have you heard?'

'He's a right one, him.'

'Do you know if he's in the area?'

'I think I saw him about twenty minutes ago.'

'Do you know where he is?'

Dad could see police trooping into Nan's. He pointed across the street: 'He went that way, I think.'

'Right, thank you.'

Dad had the girlfriend of the moment stashed around a corner. He grabbed her, jumped on a tram and was off. That was his style of stunt. He wouldn't panic and start running. He would – and could – think on his feet. He would face them up, take the mickey. He loved it.

The newspapers compared him to gentleman thief Arsène Lupin, a fictional and glamorous French criminal who'd been turned into a cartoon character when I was growing up. The people he gets the better of, with lots of style and colourful flair, are always nastier than Lupin. He's a Robin Hood-style criminal, like Raffles or 'The Saint'. Lupin! It all added to the cult revolving around Dad.

Still the press kept searching for new descriptions of him. After his next exploit he was compared in the same sentence to Lupin *and* Rocambole, another popular fictional anti-hero. *Rocambolesque* is the tag given to any kind of fantastic adventure. And Dad had many *Rocambolesque* moments.

The flamboyant publicity just brought more pressure on the cops to get Dad off the streets. Finally, in the summer of 1974, when he was twenty-five years old, they got him into Central Court on robbery charges. He was sentenced to a year in San Vittore prison, Milan's number one jail, which is renowned for its security.

Dad had as much regard for that security as he had for the law. He was *Mafiosi*. He'd been inside for only five weeks when his brother visited him. Francesco is five years younger than Dad but looks like his twin. Dad was fed up with being caged.

He and Uncle Francesco talked for a time and then Dad asked him to change sides at the visiting table, to come over and sit in the inmate's chair for a moment. And wait. In an instant Dad walked over to and out through the visitors' exit. The next thing Uncle Francesco was being taken into the slammer, to Dad's cell.

He pleaded: 'What's going on? I'm Francesco Di Giovine, not Emilio Di Giovine!'

Finally, the guards clicked. The brothers had swapped.

'I didn't know what he was doing. He was so depressed. One minute he was there, the next minute he was telling me to switch seats. And then he was gone.' That was Uncle Francesco's bumbled explanation of Dad's jailbreak, his stroll out of San Vittore, making him able to celebrate being a free man. At least a free man-on-the-run. Typical Dad.

The prison thought it was a set-up but the only person set up was Uncle Francesco. His story was dismissed and he was kept in jail for three months for aiding a jailbreak.

When Nan heard what had happened she exclaimed: 'Oh, that bloody son of mine.' No one knew whether it was praise or criticism.

For the front pages it was: *'Rocambole a San Vittore.'*

As they were writing the headlines, Dad was on a train out of the city. He went south, staying with friends, and then from Rome he made some phone calls. One was to Melanie Taylor, who had returned to England when her Continental dance tour was over.

'My sweetheart! My love! I can't live without you! I'm flying over to see you. I must be with you.'

He laid it on with a trowel. It was the perfect escape route, a ready-made safe haven. Dad moved to Huntingdon, Cambridgeshire, to link up with Melanie, and got a job at the Huntingdonshire Hotel where she worked. He'd never worked in a hotel in his life, he'd never worked legitimately, but he swiftly moved up the ranks and was appointed assistant manager in charge of a huge staff.

One evening in the bar he got into conversation with Giuseppe Salerno, who was also from Milan. Understandably, they got on well and had much to talk about. Salerno was butler to the Earl of Dartmouth, who was staying with friends in the area. Over the hotel's fine wine Dad and he became great mates. Salerno would drop in to the hotel when he could, or Dad and Melanie would visit him in London at the quiet and elegant Westbury Hotel in Clifford Street, near the Earl's Mayfair home. This was the house Giuseppe Salerno ran, and his duties included the security of the silverware storeroom. He had the key to lock it. And unlock it.

Which is what he did on a rainy November evening when the Earl was at a charity dinner.

Dad turned up, they bundled out the silver jewellery, plates and cutlery valued at £30,000. Dad drove off back to Huntingdon leaving his new friend Giuseppe tied up and gagged in the entrance hall. It looked like a perfect robbery.

It was for Dad. Not for anyone else. When the Earl returned from his evening, he found his manservant apparently assaulted and robbed, his family silver out the door. Thieves! Robbery!

Melanie helped Dad hide the silver, wrapped in blankets, in a cellar at the hotel. It would be sold when the heat died down. But Giuseppe wasn't born to crime. He wasn't injured, there was no sign of forced entry. To the police it looked as though the butler did it.

Giuseppe tripped himself up again and again during his police interviews. After yet another contradiction, he cracked. He pointed the finger at his fellow Italian and the hiding place of the silver. When the police reached the hotel they confronted Melanie. She wouldn't say where the silver was and it took them three hours to find it. They never found Dad. He was on the run again. When the Cambridge police ran the name Emilio Di Giovine past Interpol and the *carabinieri* they got an impressive criminal CV in return.

Yet by the time the case reached the Old Bailey in London on 11 August 1975, their man was long, long gone. But his lover was there. Melanie Taylor admitted 'dishonestly assisting in the removal or retention' of the stolen silver.

Judge Gwyn Morris seemed to regard her involvement as some sort of crime of passion. And, because she was acting out of 'love and loyalty', he gave her a twelve-month conditional discharge. She spoke outside the court to those bewildered by what had happened to this attractive, sensibly dressed blonde from Middle England.

'I could not give Emilio away. He told me he was a racing driver. I thought I loved him. I had even got things together for my bottom drawer for our wedding. I was duped. I can't believe it. I'll never fall for a Latin lover's charm again. I don't want to see him any more.'

She hasn't. By the time Melanie went back to live with her forgiving parents in suburbia, Dad was enlarging a business in which the value of the silver swag would be petty cash. And he was taking much more risk. Melanie won a stay-out-of-jail card. Dad was setting up drug connections throughout Europe and paying the way with other enterprises.

He was involved with his brother Antonio in supplying stolen cars to Kuwait. Members of their organisation would steal the cars in Spain and then ship them over. Officials at the port of entry in Kuwait were fixed and the cars, all expensive, powerful machines – most stolen to order – would literally sail in.

Unexpectedly, there was a payoff breakdown when a ship full of fifty cars was being taken in. There were problems with the paperwork and a Kuwaiti customs officer was arrested. The Spanish police went to town and finally implicated Dad and my uncle. They were locked away in La Modelo Prison in Barcelona in October 1976. Dad wasn't going to hang around.

He charmed himself a job in the prison hospital so he could see it how it worked – the hours, the people, guards and regulations – and how he could play it to his advantage, snitch his freedom. He'd made friends with an extravagantly connected Italian inmate, a *Mafiosi*, and got contacts for a gypsy who could help him in Barcelona if – or, in Dad's case, when – he got out. For weeks he handed out food, helped with the beds and generally made himself useful as he kept his eyes and ears on the system. He found out that if the prison doctor couldn't figure out what was wrong with an inmate he was shipped off to specialists at Santa Cru Hospital. With an armed guard. Three officers would escort the handcuffed prisoner, wearing regular street clothes so as not to upset regular patients, on the way for treatment and also guard him at the civil hospital.

Dad got very ill. A mystery ailment. The prison medics couldn't fathom what was wrong. Off he went to hospital in Barcelona. One officer stayed with the car and the other two lads escorted him into the examination room. While they were waiting for a doctor, one of the cops went out for a cigarette. Still handcuffed, Dad grabbed the other guard and quickly locked him in the toilet. Then he was off. He casually walked down the hospital corridor and out of a side entrance and into the Barcelona bustle. There were people everywhere in the middle of a hot afternoon, 7 July 1977. The seventh day of the seventh month, '77, four of a kind, 7777, a winning trick. He says he felt like Houdini.

And Dad's luck held, for as the bulls began running in Pamplona that day, he took a long route to Milan. All he had on him was one of the tiny keys you got on cans of corned beef. Dad employed that for all sorts – Fray Bentos robberies, if you like. He'd open every possible lock with those keys, and his speciality was cars. With these tricky little things he'd get a car unlocked quicker than most people could open the can.

Within a few minutes he'd jumped in a taxi and ordered it to drive to the Plaça de Catalunya, which is the busiest square in the city. He had no cash and was hiding his handcuffs so he asked the cab driver to wait while he made a phone call. He ducked into the subway and came out on the other side of the plaza, from where he could see the taxi waiting. He also saw lots of police movement. He went into a toilet and picked the lock on the cuffs. It took a moment. In the street he brazenly stopped a young woman and asked if she'd help him, let him sleep at her house, but she wasn't having any of that. Imagine! He thought his smile would be enough.

He persuaded a beggar to give him some loose change to call the gypsy contact, but there was no reply. There were a couple of Italian warships in port at Barcelona and he heard a sailor with a Calabrian accent asking for directions. Dad gave him a cock and bull story about being stranded in the city and the lad gave him a load of pesetas. Everywhere he went, he somehow talked people into helping. It was getting dark.

He chanced his luck on the last bus to the outskirts of Barcelona, a trip on which he might or might not be checked. It held again. And good fortune was his once more when he found a minibus at 3 a.m. He clicked it open with his corned beef key and had a couple of hours' kip.

But even though it was July, the winds were howling, plants were jumping off balconies and the van was rocking. It was early morning when he got to La Rambla pedestrian mall in central Barcelona, but it was packed with tourists who provided people cover. It was before 8 a.m. when he rang the gypsy, who said he'd just got in from his evening and to call back at 1 p.m.

'Hang on a minute! Look, pal, this is an emergency. I've been told you can help me ...'

He told Dad to come round, get this bus, do this, do that, take another bus, do that. The front door was opened by a Spanish gypsy who looked like a flamenco dancer. When he and his wife realised who Dad was – his picture was all over the telly – they treated him like a king. They couldn't do enough for him. This guy did robberies and Dad, the legendary 'Lupin', was one of his heroes. The guy showed him what he'd nicked, including some gold bars. While

Antonio was stuck in jail and the cops searched land, sea and air for Dad, he put his feet up with them for a week. He rested and plotted.

He always found a way to do everything. There's nothing that can't be done by my dad. A fake passport was arranged from Italy, and when it and money arrived he moved on. He took a plane from Barcelona to Madrid and then a train to Malaga and a taxi to Algeciras. From there he took the ferry to Tangiers, where he fell in with a Neapolitan–Moroccan man who entertained him while he waited for three days for the first plane to Rome.

His trail was complex but cold. A bodyguard-driver met him at Fiumicino Airport and they drove back to Milan, which with my family's efforts was developing into one of the world's most important drug-trafficking junctions. In tandem, the European 'Di Giovine Connection' was operating. It was a family business run from Piazza Prealpi, their estate, their fiefdom. My Auntie Natalina's husband Luigi Zolla was appointed by Nan as 'manager' of the Piazza.

It was recognised, if reluctantly accepted by rival drug organisations, that the Di Giovine family had majority control. Drug suppliers dealt directly and exclusively with the family or there would be trouble. When one of the family's dealers attempted to set up business for himself, Nan issued only one instruction: 'Kill him.'

He was murdered within twenty-four hours.

Another dealer didn't learn that lesson and tried to edge into Di Giovine territory. He died too.

The notoriety increased with the viciousness with which the family's dominion was protected. Intrusion was not tolerated. Business had to be protected, no matter what.

When Dad's sister Rita was sixteen years old, she was living at Nan's with her boyfriend and they started dealing heroin. When thieves brought stolen TVs and other plunder to be fenced they used the money Nan paid them in the kitchen to buy smack off Auntie Rita in the bedroom. It was a clever crime carousel. But there was a big bust-up between Rita and her boyfriend. She was weighing the heroin and cutting it with sugar to make it go further. She didn't see that as a rip-off. But she didn't like it that her boyfriend was short-changing their buyers by putting less than the correct weight of heroin mix in the drug packets.

Rita was never Nan's favourite. She was too needy, too eager to please, and Nan didn't respect her as a result. She preferred the kids who spoke out and gave the finger to authority. She didn't always treat Rita terribly well because of this, and when she found out what Rita and her boyfriend were rowing about she went ballistic. She didn't want anyone in the middle. She wanted total control. After that when the druggies brought stolen goods *she* paid them in heroin, cutting out her own daughter.

Like a medieval warlord, Nan had an official taster-tester. Only in his teens, Mimmino, who lived out back in a lean-to, wasn't employed to check the family food for poison but the strength of the heroin. His reaction to his fix would dictate whether the batch could be cut for more profit. A risky business, and he eventually died from an overdose.

There was so much heroin being packed, unpacked, cut and doctored at Nan's that a couple of neighbours, women who allowed her incoming calls on their untapped phones, were convinced their dogs were being affected, getting high on the aroma and behaving very oddly. In the mêlée of daily life no one else noticed, just gave a shrug when it was mentioned. The dogs seemed content.

Dad was making more connections with the Turkish gangs who were a developing influence in Milan. They operated easily in the shadow of Italy's kidnapping epidemic in the years after the profitable snatching of John Paul Getty III. The kidnappers targeted kids from rich families and many of the victims were never seen alive again. In 1976 more than eighty men, women and children were held to ransom. The kidnap and murder of Aldo Moro, the two-time Italian Prime Minister, in 1978 remains an open wound for Italy. But with all the scrutiny and risks and no guaranteed profit, kidnapping wasn't a business my family wanted to move into. Drugs were the future. Yet there's always friction, with other organisations wanting to expand in the same line of business. It's impossible to grow without taking up space that others believe belongs to them. There were plenty of 'others'.

Dad was mixing with a lot of evil people. One sinister gang, nicknamed Kidnaps Inc, was responsible for grabbing twenty-one hostages, three of whom vanished for ever. A

Yugoslav called Francesco Mafoda was one of the leaders. He understood Dad's contacts and influence and tried to recruit him into the organisation. This guy wasn't just ruthless and mean; he was borderline psychotic. His unsmiling, pockmarked face was a signal he wasn't a good bet. Dad said no.

Mafoda didn't like being turned down but Dad was his own man. And a free one. Nan had paid off a judge from a new bank account in Marbella, to finally get the prison swap charges dismissed. Dad fobbed off Mafoda and concentrated on the drugs business. And keeping business in the family. Along with his brothers and sisters, Dad controlled teams in Milan dealing with the Turkish shipments brought in by road, kilos and kilos of heroin often hidden in giant canisters of cooking lard. Week by week the number of trucks, buses, consignments and millions of dollars involved grew and the heroin distribution crews took on new sales teams to spread the deadly but so lucrative product.

For Dad, it was a wonderful world. And something surprising had happened in his life. He was in love. Adele Rossi was only sixteen years old when Dad started dating her. He adored her. She went everywhere with him. He guarded her, looked after her, loved her. They went around hand in hand. They were always touching each other. Not in a sexual way but as though they were making sure the other one was still there; seeing wasn't enough. She met Mum and me and we liked her. She was lovely, a joyful personality. And beautiful, with long legs and a cascade of blonde hair. Everyone noticed how happy Dad was. He was even happier when Adele got pregnant. And I was delighted, and nervous, at the prospect of having a sister.

In this absurd world, Mum, estranged and separated from her husband, was also trying to have a romantic life but Dad's power and personality were an ongoing obstruction. He didn't want to be with Mum but he didn't want anyone else to be with her either. It was ridiculous but so common in broken relationships. Dad didn't love Mum in that way, didn't want to be with her, but was jealous at the thought that someone else might pay her attention.

Some confused and irate husbands might make idle threats if any other man got close to their wife, estranged or not, but with Dad it would have been action not threats. With him so close by, how could Mum ever find happiness again? What man would want to be with her and play surrogate daddy to his little girl when he knew Dad was around the corner? One guy, Gianni, decided he couldn't live with the risk of reprisals for getting close to Mum and me, and he broke off their relationship.

Mum did see other people, including one guy who was a friend of the family so they had to keep him all hush-hush from Dad. One night he stayed over at the Mussolini flat with its one big room with one big bed. Mum slept on one side, I slept in the middle, and this guy was on the other side. I was seven years old and slept in pyjamas. I didn't have any underwear on. I woke up in the middle of the night and this guy's hand was between my legs, on me. He wasn't messing.

It was just there. Plonked on it. What could have happened if I hadn't woken up? I was lucky he didn't do anything more.

I pushed his hand away and cuddled up to Mum. I never told anybody. What if I had mentioned it to Nan or my dad? Well, Mum might not be alive. I'm not kidding when I say that. Dad would have taken me from her, chopped the guy's hands off and killed him.

I can't condemn Mum. She only wanted some personal happiness, as did Dad, but both in their own ways. Yet Dad had changed. Breaking his own rules about business and pleasure, for that's all that women had meant before, he took Adele along to his meetings. One evening, on 2 October 1977, he got a call about a heroin shipment worth around £50,000 to the family; nothing to be concerned about, a simple distribution deal. He arranged to meet the contact man, Vittorio Bosisio, at a local coffee shop to make the arrangements for the next day's delivery.

Unknown to Dad, Vittorio Bosisio was a dead man walking. He had run up hard against a brutal, no-nonsense Yugoslav called Mimmo Pompeo who carried machine pistols like cowboy six-guns. Bosisio hadn't paid off on a drug shipment and Pompeo issued an order to take him out. But Vittorio Bosisio, hard-faced and streetwise, was crafty and had kept himself alive for three months. Now he needed money, needed a deal. And someone tipped off the Slav where he'd be that evening at 9 p.m.

No one knew that Dad and Adele would be there too. They and Bosisio ordered three double espressos, water and a biscotti each on the side, and were talking quietly when the first spray of automatic fire riddled the windows. The Slavs were determined Bosisio would die. There were eight gunmen firing from behind a line of parked cars. A thunderous rat-a-tat sounded as bullets howled into the cafe. Vittorio Bosisio took the full blast of the assault and his body was punctured from head to toe.

Adele tried to escape by running out of the front door but she rushed headlong into the guns. She was shot in the head, killed instantly, spilling on to the pavement. She'd just turned seventeen years old and was three months pregnant.

Dad acted instinctively, turning his body and throwing his hands up in front of himself, trying to block the gunfire. A barrage of bullets caught him in the arms and legs. The blood spurted and he collapsed onto the tiled floor in a coma, near death.

When the police teams arrived, they arrested him.

CHAPTER FIVE
GUNS AND ROSES

'In the middle of difficulty lies opportunity.'

ALBERT EINSTEIN

Dad woke up with flowers and a detective by the side of his hospital bed. The *investigatore di polizia* was there to see that no harm came to him. The flowers were from Mimmo Pompeo, who was concerned about his own protection since he had ordered the shooting. Adele's death and Dad's almost-fatal injuries were collateral damage. He and young Adele were not meant to have been there. The floral arrangement was a message of apology.

Sorry for killing your pregnant girlfriend.

Sorry for shooting you full of holes.

And, probably, sorry for not finishing you off. Which would have happened if not for emergency surgery and clever doctors.

The police didn't have to think like Sherlock Holmes to realise that, when he fully recovered, a bunch of roses wasn't going to be enough to calm Dad down – he wanted revenge. Vendetta? He wanted a massacre. Adele was the love of dad's life. He was devastated by her violent death.

On the front pages were photographs of her blood-soaked body splayed across the ground, a pregnant, teenage victim of mobster gunplay in central Milan, and it made provocative and controversial news. It sparked heavyweight political pressure from Rome. This was a national scandal. Something had to be done, lessons learned, the usual useless political claptrap.

Still, with Rome on their backs, the authorities in Milan were determined to prevent open warfare between the Yugoslavs and the Di Giovines. They wanted no more bodies on the streets, no further voter-upsetting mob mayhem in the newspapers.

They'd arrested Dad in the aftermath of the killings and now they charged him with a string of old robberies and burglaries. They dug up anything they could from the unsolved files to convict him, to stop revenge shootings by getting 'Lupin' off the street. They had him bang to rights on the robbery of furs and artwork worth several hundred thousand pounds from Countess Marzotto Trissino's villa near Verona. He wasn't happy about that. Unknown to Dad, his brother Francesco had photographed the proceeds of their burglary and sent the snaps to the Countess demanding a ransom. That wasn't smart, and the enraged Countess immediately blew the whistle. Dad and Francesco were identified as thieves, so there was one genuine problem in the long but generally token charge list waiting when he was carried into court on a stretcher and laid out next to the dock.

I was seven years old, but that moment is a locked memory card. It was scary for me at the back of the courtroom where I sat with Nan. I kept grabbing her hand. She kept telling me quietly not to worry, not to fuss.

Dad had a beard and long hair and was on a stretcher wearing a white gown covering his bullet-punctured body. It was the first time I had seen him since the shooting.

He looked like Jesus. Appropriately, for the plan was to crucify him.

He was so red-eyed and pale and lost-looking, I wanted to jump over the wooden railings and get to him. I just wanted to hold on to my dad. I never wanted to lose him. It was then, at that moment, when I was seven years old, that a lifetime love, a precious bond, was forged. There was a strange, psychic thing. He hadn't made eye contact with me up to that point, but then, as my emotions were boiling over, he looked straight at me. While the judge was sentencing him to return to San Vittore prison for a year, Dad smiled and blew me a kiss.

As he was stretchered from the courtroom by two armed guards, he craned his neck and gave me another smile, blew a second kiss and mouthed: '*Spiacente* [sorry].'

I was no longer just his little princess. I was his Mafia Princess. I would do anything for him.

Nan murmured to me: 'Don't worry.'

She could afford to be relaxed. She knew there wasn't going to be too much hardship. She had made arrangements for Dad to have his favourite foods in jail and any wine he wanted. He'd also have drugs and cigarettes, but not for his own use – he never touched them. The cigarettes were the pennies and pounds of prison, dope of any kind the top currency, to barter and bribe.

Of course, I did worry. Mum was not there with the rest of the family for the court case. She'd already decided she'd had enough of our life in Milan. While Dad was locked up in San Vittore we travelled to Blackpool and stayed with her mum and dad and my auntie Jill. We hung on longer than our usual trips because Mum wanted to see how I would take to life in the UK, but I got physically ill because I was so desperately homesick for Italy, for the family.

When Dad got out of jail in November 1978, it wasn't a game of Happy Families. I hardly saw him and never knew when I would again. He was totally single-minded about business. And ruthless. Adele's killing had hardened him even more. He ploughed everything into narcotics smuggling, operating with the Turks to bring in even more heroin. The deals were running into multiple multiples of tens of thousands of pounds. Sometimes a week, always a month.

It didn't take long for the clock to turn to High Noon. There were other just as determined people as the Di Giovine family. There were gun battles over territory, beatings and killings, and one death led to another and, of course, there was the vendetta. The Yugoslavs were the big threat and Adele's death still had to be avenged. All I knew of it was that Dad seemed distant most of the time. He didn't seem to have as much time for me, for anyone.

The family concluded what they called 'the negotiations' in a territorial battle that ended with five of the Slav gang dead in a week.

The Di Giovine enterprise, like the drug supply, was endless, and there were always new customers, always the search for more outlets. Patricia Di Giovine, my mum, on the other hand, was searching for an escape. In the August of 1979 we went on holiday to another world, to Calabria, and stayed with my nan's family. She had relatives, brothers and sisters and their families, throughout the area. My god-father, Uncle Demitri Serraino, was our main host, the patriach. He was lovely, a nice, very particular, elegant man and a bit of a lad. His wife Lidia couldn't have kids and they'd fed her with hormones that made her really hairy; she looked like a man and had a smell like a man as well. Mum and I had to stay at her house. She was lovely to talk to, but she had bushy hairs under her chin and she used to get Mum to pluck them out.

I sat there worrying: 'Oh my God, please don't let me have to pull out the hairs.' I dreaded the thought of it.

Uncle Demitri and the Calabrian family were set in their old-world ways, their attitudes as ingrown as Lidia's chin hairs. Nan had bought land, and her brother and his wife, Uncle Giuseppe and Auntie Milina, kept rabbits on some of her acres, which were near their farm. Auntie Milina was unpleasant to everybody and I couldn't stand her. They told me she could kill people with her bare hands; she was a *generale in gonnella*, a general in a skirt.

One day I went across to the farm where they kept the pigs and these gorgeous rabbits. Just as she was killing a rabbit for our tea, I pleaded, 'Please don't kill that white one!'

But she killed it right in front of me. Just battered his head, and skinned it. It was awful. I'll never forget it.

I cried and asked: 'What are you going to do with the skin?'

Auntie Milina held it out to me and said, 'You can make a pair of knickers if you want.'

It was horrible. I was miserable, fed up with that. Nan tried to cheer me up as we sat by the olive groves, fanned by the gusts of *zagarna,* orange blossom breeze. She said Dad might visit on Thursday. That brought a smile to my face. It seemed so long since I'd seen him. I didn't want to get too excited in case he didn't turn up but I couldn't help myself. I counted to one hundred and then one hundred again to make the time go faster.

He appeared in the early evening, and as I ran into his arms he said he had come specially to see me. He hadn't brought any presents or luggage – no change of clothes, no toothbrush. All he was carrying was a Benelli 12-gauge shotgun.

The next morning after breakfast he took me out to learn how to use that big gun, with its worn stock and oiled barrels. He carried the weapon slung over his shoulder on a loose, tan leather strap. The red shells he gave me to load the shotgun were warm from his pocket. He stopped me with a gentle smile when I tried to put in more than five cartridges. It was a nice grin, but faraway, not familiar.

We were out near the olive groves, close to orchards of lemon and lime. My face was flushed with the heat and excitement, cooled only a little by the breeze with the orange bouquet from the bergamot trees.

I had to concentrate on the lesson. When I'd loaded the gun he explained that each shell was packed not with pellets but with a single, rifled slug of lead.

'What's the difference?' I asked.

He explained that pellets can catch game birds from the sky, while one spinning slug would bring down a charging wild boar. Stop it in its tracks.

The shotgun was difficult, too heavy for me to handle properly. He smiled and I could see the squinty white lines around his eyes where the sun hadn't reached. He shouldered it. With a soft click, he slid the safety catch off, pulled me out of his line of fire, and blasted several times into the distance, at targets of his imagination. Acrid cordite masked the orange blossom, as I clapped applause at my baptism of gunfire.

My father put his strong, tanned arm around me and I could feel his breath in my right ear as he whispered: *'Amo la mia piccola principessa.'* ['I love my little princess.']

My heart swelled. I adored him. I would do anything for him, anything he wanted. He only had to ask. And then later that day he was gone. Just like that.

There were no explanations from Nan, and Mum avoided talking about him. That was typical now. She always spoke about 'the two of us' and finding a nice place to stay. I wanted us all to be together as a family. I loved my dad. I wanted us to stay with him, or near him at least.

We returned to Milan at the end of the month but I didn't go back to class. I was going to another school. Our bags were packed, our whole life in Italy in six cases. Mum was more than ready to leave Milan, leave Dad and Nan and all the Serraino–Di Giovine family and connections, to leave their underworld, the *malavita*. Dad was mad about it but there was nothing he could do. Mum had made up her mind and deep down I think he knew it would be better for me to get away as there was so much violence going on.

When Nan hugged and kissed me goodbye, it didn't feel right. I knew she didn't want me to leave her and, inside myself, I never did. I was upset and I didn't want to go, but Mum made much of the novelty of living in England. And there'd be a nice new school. It would be fun, like another holiday. She was trying to convince herself that it was not just the only plan but also the best plan.

It was a sunny morning in early September 1979 when we left Milan. A day later our train rolled through the rain at Fishergate Hill and along platform five at Preston Station. My mum's older sister Auntie Jill met us and I remember she had brought a spare Marks and Sparks umbrella to keep us dry in our scamper with our stuff to the car park. We moved into Auntie Jill and Uncle Adrian's detached house on a very posh new estate in Carlton, Lancashire. Mum had already written to the local authority from Milan and got us on the council house list but Auntie Jill would have let us stay forever. Despite trying, she and my uncle didn't have any children of their own so they were happy to spoil me rotten. I loved the attention but also the space and the constant hot water. Baths – hot baths! – were part of the day, not a dream. I was given my own bedroom but for more than six months I still slept in Mum's bed because at only nine years old I was scared of my new world.

I kept wondering about Dad, where he was, and when, if, he was going to come and see me. I would dream about him and look at pictures and photographs and wonder if that's where he was. I would see a photo of a building and wonder if he'd walked past it. I was constantly searching for something to give me a connection to him.

As a little girl you need reassurance. I wanted my dad to tell me he loved me. I adored him. I loved him. I would tell him. Why wouldn't he speak to me, tell me he loved me? But for this little girl there was no point in tantrums. I knew stamping my foot would get me nowhere: *L'albero vecchio non si drizza piu* [An old tree cannot be made straight].

But time played its part and I began to settle. Auntie Jill had a budgie called Joey, which used to sit in its cage saying, 'Hello, I'm Joey Sheppard.'

My uncle and I liked to play a game where we waited until Mum and Auntie Jill were talking thirteen to the dozen and we'd open Joey's cage and he'd zing out. Joey's flight plan was always directly to Auntie Jill's head. She used so much spray her hair was like a helmet and Joey would land without her even noticing. He'd sit there, perched on her head, and she'd be talking and talking. It was only when Mum collapsed in a fit of laughter that she realised and chased me around the house.

We'd go to Blackpool for the day and walk along the beach and throw stones into the sea. Dinner-time specials were fish and chips and caramel puddings. It was all so simple, normal, a different life.

But also a different language. I didn't speak more than a few words of English. When I was first given Smarties I thought they were counters, not sweets. I couldn't write English or count in English or understand lessons in English, which means that the staff at Carlton Green Primary School must have been fantastic because I flourished there. The teachers gave me plenty of attention, one-to-one classes, and so a couple of years later when I went to Hodgson High School, where Mum had gone to school, I'd caught up with the others. In fact, I was better at English than most kids my age.

I cherished the school uniform Mum laid out on my bed every morning. Wearing the grey skirt, bright blue sweater and blue and grey tie made me feel important. I'd never worn a tie before and I felt smarter and grown up.

I just had to get stuck into finding my English self. Up until then I'd talked and thought in Italian, but now I had to operate in a different language and culture, be a Lancashire lass. At that age I was like a sponge with all the new information. What made me work harder was wanting not to be different, wanting to fit in, to be a little girl like the other little girls, and not just to talk like the other girls but to *sound* like them; to belong.

Of course, all the kids were interested in me for the very fact I was different. They'd ask me to teach them swear words in Italian and then parrot them around the playground. I could now swear in two languages. And fight. I was popular and I could hold my own. I had a couple of scraps at primary school but nothing too serious.

The most upsetting scrap was when someone I trusted, thought was a true friend, turned on me. I really didn't know what hit me. My understanding was that nobody did that, it was against the rules. She was a big girl and said: 'I'm the strongest of the class.'

Because she was my friend, I was soft. I asked: 'How do you know that?'

She showed me by punching me. It was the last year of primary. The kids were running around the playground chanting: 'Fight, fight, fight.' Maybe she wanted to put on a show for them for she was mean. She bashed me. She hit me properly, really hard, knocked me to the ground and sat on my belly, then slapped me a couple of times. I was shocked that my friend could hurt me like that.

The next day I was doubled up in pain. She wasn't *that* tough. It turned out I had to have my appendix out, but Mum always swore it was because of her attack.

Once when I was thirteen I caught a girl my age beating up an eleven-year-old girl against a wall. I grabbed the bully and got hold of her neck and pushed her up the wall and demanded, 'How do you like this? If I ever catch you doing that again, I'll do far more than put you up the wall.' I couldn't stand anything like that because I knew what it felt like.

As I got older, if someone was horrid to me I might be a bitch right back but I never went out of my way to be nasty for no reason or just for the sake of it. I was loud and a bit naughty at school but I didn't get a lot of detentions because I seemed to get away with things. I could have done far better academically. I wasn't lazy. I was just too busy with my life. Too busy with my make-up, getting my clothes right, being a teenage girl. I wasn't thick but I wasn't very academic. I was good at sports and represented the school in javelin and discus competitions, but I wasn't enthusiastic about it. There were other things running around – boys.

Mum found work as a chambermaid; it didn't pay well but with all the seafront hotels in Blackpool there were plenty of hours on offer. Within a year of returning we'd moved into our own rented place in Poulton-le-Fylde, and although we didn't have a lot we had our own life. Yet I still dreamed of life in Italy and wondered about my dad. Would he call? Would he visit? I missed him, I missed life in Milan.

So I couldn't believe it when some of that life turned up on our doorstep in England. From nowhere Grandpa Rosario arrived to see us with Auntie Rita's husband Uncle Lino in early 1980. Their visit wasn't expected so it was even more exciting for me. I loved seeing Grandpa for he'd always been around, the next best thing to Dad. This was a treat and there was plenty of cash for it. Grandpa was a changed man. Gone was the usual country look and in its place he wore a sharp suit with designer accessories. Uncle Lino, who I was wary of, was his stylish twin.

Grandpa said he was taking me to see the Queen. And we did go to Buckingham Palace but he said she wasn't home that day. We stayed in a smart West End hotel, all the bills paid in cash, and visited other tourist spots like the Tower of London. It was five-star all the way. Grandpa had a couple of people to see but most of his attention was on us. I asked Mum how we could afford all these things but she smiled and said not to fuss.

Before he left Grandpa gave Mum hundreds of pounds: 'Go out and get yourself and Marisa some clothes.'

When I realised Grandpa was leaving I was devastated; I was longing to visit Italy and see my family. Mum saw it in my face: 'Don't worry. We'll go back to visit everyone when the holidays come around. It won't be long.'

She missed Nan and all her friends as well, but she made it clear our life was in England now. All Mum cared about was that I settled down safely and did well at school. All her attention, time and money were devoted to me. Hers wasn't a money-rich lifestyle but she had me and was absolutely determined I would be well brought up, an English princess. She still made a point of speaking to me in Italian, because that was very much part of my life too. For all her hurt she didn't want me to lose that link. It worked. When I speak Italian, I think Italian, and it's exactly the same when I speak English. The idiom changes. I change. It's far more complex than driving on the left or driving on the right. You're not changing sides, you're splitting a personality.

When we went down to the beach at weekends for a wander around, I would sometimes look out to the Irish Sea and imagine Dad sailing in, taking the long way as ever. I said as much to Mum but she just frowned and said, 'Marisa, Daddy is busy.'

He was. He was on the run, a fugitive in America. In the months since we left Italy, the drug business in Milan had escalated and so had the battle for power and profit. My family was at the centre of it and deals were being conjured all the time.

Francesco Mafoda, one of the leaders of Kidnaps Inc, the man who had unsuccessfully tried to recruit Dad, had a lean, elegant style. He didn't look like a thick-necked Iron Curtain hoodlum but that was always his approach. His organisation had realised drugs were more profitable and less risky a game than kidnapping, and that they didn't provoke so many head-lines. The Di Giovine family and especially Emilio Di Giovine were a huge obstacle to Mafoda's mob creating one drug empire. The word around the city was that Mafoda had put out a contract on Dad, which Dad found really offensive. Not that Mafoda had tendered for his death. But he'd only put a small amount on his head. He boasted: 'I'm worth a million at least!'

Yet he knew he couldn't be protected 24/7 and some smacked-out junkie with a gun could take him out. And would for a lot less money. There were also the young mob guns who would take a chance as much for the prestige – making their name, their *cojones* – as the money. Whatever the bravado, his life was on the line.

And Mafoda pissed Dad off even more. He tried to negotiate, got cheeky. He said he'd stop the contract if the Di Giovines gave him a giant share of the action in Piazza Prealpi. And allowed him majority control of all drugs operations.

'Kill the bastard,' was Nan's view when she and Dad talked about the threat from the Slav gangster. Nan had no second thoughts about how to resolve it. She wanted to protect the family business – but also her son.

She didn't rush things. Like some wily spycatcher, she deliberated and weighed up what would resolve the problem and prompt more profit in the future. Certainly, arrangements had to be made to get Mafoda out of the way, to defuse or eliminate him. There was a lot on top of Dad, a great deal of pressure from the police and the Slavs. Mafoda was sneaking around, stirring things up between different groups. He created bad blood between Dad and a big gangster family from Puglia, the stiletto heel of Italy. The Puglia crew were dealing in huge amounts of drugs and Mafoda was telling them one thing and Dad another. The gang leaders both realised how dangerous the Slav was: not just to them but to their worldwide operations. Mafoda was a crazy guy, capable of doing anything, and mad enough to believe he was untouchable.

He did not consider Nan a threat, though. Nan? This matriarchal lady who looked like an ageing housewife? What threat was she? She didn't want trouble, did she?

Nan got word to Mafoda spelling out something like that. The family didn't want any bloodshed, there was enough business to go round and Mafoda must consider himself a friend of the Di Giovine family for life. His friends were the Di Giovine's friends, his enemies the Di Giovine's enemies. It was the beginning of a beautiful partnership.

It was classic *malavita*-speak yet Mafoda didn't see it, his vision tinted by his arrogance. He regarded his play as a triumph, a result. He had what he wanted without fear of reprisals from the family or the police if he hit Dad. He should celebrate. He *would* celebrate. What about the bar on the far corner of the Piazza, headquarters of the empire he would be involved in running? Ennobled by his self-belief and a celebratory bottle of red wine, Mafoda wandered towards the Piazza Prealpi.

Nan wanted Dad out of the way before anything terminal happened, to get to America and boost the 'Di Giovine Connection' in New York where there were many family friends. Dad was keen to get there for altogether different reasons. There was business and there was Fanny, a statuesque Moroccan–Italian who provided him with exotic evening entertainments. He had broken off his affair with Effie, Miss Paraguay, but she was always tracking him down, telling him in her ladylike way that she was heartbroken and they must always be together.

Fanny was far more fun in every possible way. Gorgeous, she had the added attraction of liking money rather than questions. She was Dad's perfect woman. But she'd taken off for New York and set herself up in a Manhattan apartment. Dad was missing her tricks.

Nan, who despaired of Dad's love life and thought he was still under the spell of Miss Paraguay, had started her plan to get him to America a couple of weeks earlier. Connections. As long as I've known them, the family could always get paperwork, false documents for any purpose. At a price. There wasn't anyone with influence, an official or an intermediary, a shopkeeper or a wine merchant, they hadn't corrupted. It didn't matter whether it was dodgy passports or prime Dolcelatte, they got the best.

A passport was created in the name of Nan's brother Lorenzo Serraino. It was Dad's face that looked out from the photograph page. An associate took it to Palermo in Sicily where it was 'approved' and a visa issued for America. Unlike most things in Palermo, that passport and visa were incorruptible, the real thing. Well, almost.

With the passport in Milan, his money belt loaded with dollars and Pan Am tickets booked for the night flight to New York, all Dad had to do on 12 June 1980 was get on the plane. He was delayed. He couldn't find the new passport.

While others searched and finally found it he was hanging around at Nan's. He'd walked across the square to visit and say goodbye to his brother Antonio, whose wife, Livia De Martino, was expecting a baby. He was outside their apartment when his minder Carlo – with all the threats, Dad was armed and wanted an extra pair of eyes constantly checking around him – saw Mafoda across the street. Mafoda's red face seemed even brighter against his beige, rather rumpled linen suit.

My mum, Pat, with her first love, the gorgeous Alessandro, at Milan's open-air swimming pool in 1968.

My dad, Emilio, looking very much part of the 1970s with his 'tache.

That's six-month-old me, with Dad in Milan.

Marlboro Girl! On the cigarette smuggling runs between Italy and Switzerland with Dad and Mum.

February 1971, going it alone as a smuggler with the giant packs of cigarettes. Dad was taking the picture so I wasn't alone with the smokes!

The curly ringlets had gone, thanks to the nits and Mum's scissors, but that's me (far left) with my friends in October 1974.

A winter wonderland in Switzerland on one of the cigarette runs.

Summer 1976, and I still wasn't too big for Mum to lift me up in her arms.

With the snow dusting the mountains in the background that's me with Mum and my aunties Mariella and Mima.

Carnival day with my Spanish señorita look – and I had one fan! In my hand.

In the hills of Reggio Calabria with Dad when he took me out shooting. That's when he whispered to me, *'Amo la mia piccola principessa'* ('I love my little princess').

Visitors came from around the world, including Mafia dons and soldiers, for the mountain parade in the Calabrian hills every summer. This is our family after taking part in 1980.

Guns and Dolls: Nan in a surprisingly racy pose in her guest bedroom in Milan with my cousin – not Auntie – Rita, visiting from Calabria at Easter, 1981. I'm in the background 'armed' with my toys.

Girls on the
balcony:
Aunties
Angela, Mima
and Lidia.
That's me
on the right
with my arm
around Nan.

England: my
English
grandma's
birthday,
18 November 1982.
Grandma,
Aunties
Sharon and
Jill, Mum,
me and baby
cousin
Caroline.

Italy:
the other
side of my
family,
another
world. Reggio
Calabria in
1981 and I'm
with my nan's
sister Nunzia
and my great
grandma
Margherita.

Again, my two worlds living and looking at life in such a different way: with Nan at her home in Milan in 1986 ...

... and, on the same balcony three years later, with Mum.

'Oh, *compadre*!' Carlo shouted loudly to the Slav so Dad would look out and see who it was.

Mafoda always carried a gun, always, always had one on him. When he turned around he pulled something out of his jacket and my dad whipped his pistol from its holster and shot him. Across the road from Nan's house, he killed him with a single bullet.

That's when they found it was a bunch of car keys Mafoda had pulled from his pocket. He was armed, he had a gun. But he'd pulled out the key chain.

Not a gun.

Dad didn't like what happened but at the same time he knew Mafoda was a very dangerous guy who wasn't all there. Anything could have gone down. He thought Mafoda was drawing his pistol to assassinate him. The cops do it all the time – shooting people who aren't carrying guns or bombs but who they think are. It wasn't much different for my dad. I know that this guy had tooled himself up and gone to the area to kill my dad. My dad knew and he was ready.

Dad and Carlo didn't have time to analyse what had happened. Dad had to make that flight. They whisked him away. He grabbed his travel stuff from Nan's – no time for more farewells – and was in the car with Carlo putting his foot hard to the pedal and heading to Malpensa Airport.

And Dad's flight on to New York.

Where the most powerful Mafia family in America were going to help him start an astonishing, if dangerous, new life.

CHAPTER SIX
COUNT MARCO AND THE DAPPER DON

*'When it's three o'clock in New York
it's still 1938 in London.'*

BETTE MIDLER

Mum knew Dad was on the run but, like the police and Interpol, thought he was hiding out in Morocco or Portugal. He'd always escaped into Europe or North Africa in the past. She thought he'd just appear, as he always had, and dismissed my questions about him coming to see me with the usual: 'He's busy, Marisa, don't worry about him.'

It wasn't just me who was thinking about Dad. After Mafoda's death the international alarm bells were ringing for him. He'd vanished, like Lupin, as if by magic. Other than Nan and Grandpa and a couple of his brothers, no one knew where Dad was. The cops had issued a warrant for his arrest on murder charges. Yes, he'd pulled the trigger, but it hadn't gone down the way they were telling it. He needed to become a new man to keep his freedom and take control of the American arm of the spiralling family drug empire.

When he arrived at JFK Airport the first thing he thought of was a safe haven and exotic home comforts. He phoned Fanny and she was glad to hear his voice. She also had a surprise – she was pregnant by him. He was delighted with the news. An instant family was wonderful cover for the soon-to-be-ennobled man on the run. Dad was about to live out the later chapters of *The Count of Monte Cristo*. And they would be equally exciting, involving murder, kidnapping and death, greed, corruption and the politics of powerful families.

He placed his passport in a bank safety deposit box, temporarily burying Lorenzo Serraino. When he emerged from CitiBank on 2nd Avenue, he hailed a taxi as Count Marco Carraciolo, an Italian émigré, a glamorous aristocrat. He then arranged for Count Marco to have his own, personalised face. The Park Avenue plastic surgeon who worked on and around Dad's eyes and cheekbones changed his appearance to the casual glance but not for too much scrutiny. But $20,000 paid for enough work that he'd never be recognised from the old wanted posters circulated by the Italian cops through Interpol. Count Marco appeared brighter-faced, a little fresher than Emilio Di Giovine, with a couple of years trimmed from his age.

But he was not the front of Dad's Manhattan restaurant, Palio, on 57th and 2nd Avenue. It was licensed to Fanny's brother Emo but Dad bankrolled the popular eating establishment he named after the Palio of Siena bareback horse races. He had an uncanny ability in the hospitality trade and was as successful as a Manhattan restaurateur as he had been as a hotelier in England. The huge difference was that in Manhattan it was the Mob and not Fortnum & Mason who were his main suppliers.

New York knew Dad as Count Marco but he was respected for himself by the Gambino family, who were still enjoying the legacy of the man who had been the most powerful don in the United States. Carlo Gambino, the 'boss of bosses' of the American Mafia, had died from a heart attack four years earlier in 1976. The author Mario Puzo modelled his 'Godfather' on Gambino, whose mild-mannered, often decrepit appearance was deceiving and generally deadly. He never raised his voice but his soft-spoken words were Mafia law in America.

His son, Joey Gambino, was a superb connection for my family. He and Grandpa Rosario had used the same Puerto Rican crews in drug-trafficking operations. Joey leaned more towards the business than the brutality side of the Gambino rackets.

The rising star of the Gambino organisation was John Gotti, the 'Dapper Don', who favoured handmade suits and fine wine, and threatened anyone he suspected of disloyalty: 'I'll blow your house up.' He was old-style Mafia, quite prepared to 'take off the velvet glove' at what he believed were important corporate moments. That was another connection with Dad. They'd both had to carve out their prestige within their mobs.

In 1979 Gotti had been made a *capo* in return for 'good works' – basically, the execution of rival gangster James McBratney who, with a group of other mobsters, had kidnapped and murdered the Don's nephew Emmanuel 'Manny' Gambino. McBratney was the only one to escape the cops, and the Don ordered him dead. He was shot three times at point-blank range in Snoope's Bar & Grill on Staten Island on 22 May 1973. Gotti was convicted of the killing but when he got out of Green Haven maximum security in Storm-ville, New York, he was rewarded with promotion.

Dad was friendly with Gambino underboss Aniello Dellacroce and would also eat out with the main man, the *caporegime*, Paul 'Big Paulie' Castellano, to whom he became close. He looked up to him for his organisational abilities, and Castellano returned that respect to Dad. He'd see them and Gotti at the Ravenite Social Club on Mulberry Street in Little Italy. Gotti ran a meat supply company and also controlled food warehouses. He and Dad became partners in crime and cuisine: Palio was supplied by Mob shops and butchers at a special price.

There was much behind-the-scenes Gambino politics going on but, as Dad saw it, that was not his concern at the time. He liked their attitude: business was business. Personalities only played a part if they got in the way of business. When Dad arrived in the long, hot summer of 1980 the *Mafiosi* influence was overwhelming and touched almost every business, from high fashion to Wall Street, gambling and the movies, from hotels to the docks. It was all about investment: steal the money any way you can, clean it up, launder it, and bank it where the interest was high and the tax consequences zero. I don't know how they did it but it was sometimes less than zero – they got a 'bonus' just for being the bank's customers.

The old favourites included car-thieving rings, construc-tion and the garment industries, but at the start of the 1980s there was no question from anyone that the huge money then and in the future was in drugs. The legit operations were a veneer over where they were making their real money. Like all tiers of the Gambino Family, Gotti had his placement in the New York Police Department. The NYPD acted as an early warning system about any interest shown from Europe in the fugitive Emilio Di Giovine, which gave Dad lots of room and he took full advantage of his freedom to operate. It was the start of the 1980s, the consumerism heyday decade, and the Mob's drug trade thinking mirrored Wall Street's motto: 'Greed is Good'.

Whatever they wanted, my family has always gone to the source. Initially they dealt with the middlemen, but they always stepped over them. Those guys couldn't do much about it. They weren't earning money, so it was tough. It was dog eat dog. But that's how it was.

Huge consignments of heroin and cocaine were coming into Milan from Morocco as well as Turkey. The Turkish connection set up by Dad was lavish: our family used to steal cars, set them up with false documents as 'ringers' and send them back to Istanbul as part-payment. The Turks' love of high-powered vehicles heightened our profit margin. Simultaneously, the Moroccans were sending as many if not more kilos again as the Turks. The deal was so good there was a traffic snarl-up when Italian dealers became overwhelmed by the supply.

It worked for the family: America was screaming for the stuff and the market there commanded much better prices, sometimes double the European tariff. Nan as *capa* – the Lady Boss – and Grandpa and the family organised the cutting and shipping of the drugs. Operational HQ was, as always, Piazza Prealpi. Count Marco was the distribution kingpin in New York.

The smuggling operation had an elaborate beginning at the Piazza Prealpi. There and in surrounding garages, cellophane-wrapped individual kilos of heroin would be subdivided into packets of double-sided tape and plastic, which would fit in empty bottles of shampoo, hair conditioner and body lotion – the kind of toiletries you'd find in an airline passenger's luggage. The pack was Sellotaped to the inside of the container and the shampoo or conditioner or body lotion would be poured back in. They used any beauty products. A woman would carry five or six at a time. It was very straightforward. And successful. And kept in the family, for at the start the budget was tight. Relatives would get no money but a free flight to America carrying maybe £100,000 worth of drugs in their bags. That value was before Dad got it, cut it and, driving up the price to benefit from the demand, sold it to suppliers across the United States.

There were scores of 'drug tourists'. They were almost always women, mums with babies, grandmas off to visit family and single girls off to America to find or make their fortune. What they all shared, along with their prepared stories, was their extra-strong perfume to confuse drug-sniffing dogs at customs. Often they'd wear body belts that were custom-made to take half-kilo and three-quarter-kilo bags of heroin on the way out and packs of US dollars on the way back. The smack was inside the thinnest of plastic film. The belt was made out of cloth to absorb body sweat so it wouldn't slip down at a wrong moment. No one wanted a belt stuffed with heroin around their ankles at American customs. One courier was very unlucky. By the time she landed in Italy, her flesh and the money belt tape's super-glue had somehow melted together. Her body, her flesh was stuck to the cash. Olive oil and lotions did no good. She was flayed alive under a scalding shower to separate her from the money. For the *Mafiosi*, it was needs must.

Dad was running America, Nan was controlling Italy and Uncle Antonio was in charge of the Spanish Connection. But it was in New York where everything was absolutely dandy, with such an ever-upward-moving market and the Gambino family protection. An incredible amount of cash was being generated. So much money Nan was running out of places to stash it. She had heroin in her neighbours' washing powder packets and cash in their bedroom drawers. She had 'mules' moving money as well as drugs, and accounts were being opened around the world. Yet Nan remained Nan, cooking lunch and shouting at the ones she loved.

Mum and I saw the incredible change in the family's circumstances on our annual visits every August: they were living like millionaires. We were the poor English relations. Flights to Italy were expensive so we had to go by train, down to London, on to Calais and beyond to Italy. We'd go overnight. We couldn't afford a sleeper. We sat in the carriage – one of those four-each-side, facing-each-other jobs – with everyone else. You could get out into the corridor for a stretch. It was a long night. In Milan we'd meet up with everyone and after a couple of days take off for Calabria and visit the usual suspects – of whom there were more than ever. Everyone seemed to be involved.

Nan now owned most of the village of San Sperato, and Mum and I stayed in a two-storey house she had there. Her brothers still looked after the family-owned farmland but were also dealing with the heroin shipments arriving from Morocco by container ship into the port of Gioia Tauro.

San Sperato was Nan's summer headquarters. Her deckchair was in the same place every day, higher than the rest by the edge of the sand, and she sat there in a modest black swimsuit, wrapping a sarong round her legs whenever she stood up. She was under a parasol to shade her from the hot sun while we tried to cool off in the 40-degree heat by splashing about in the sea. People walking on the beach would stop by Nan's chair, stoop down and kiss her hand. Wherever she went in Reggio Calabria – the market, the shops, the doctor's – she was received with enormous respect. Doors were constantly opened, hands were always shaken and hats tipped.

There was a daily restaurant reservation for thirty of us for lunch on the beach, and the lobster and wine were waiting to nibble and sip as the orders were taken. I wondered where Dad was, but if I asked the answer was always: 'Your papa is taking care of business.'

I felt as though I was in limbo. What was I? Italian? English? I didn't really understand who I was, never mind what to think. But I knew in Italy that I was different.

A few of my English friends knew that my family was a bit dodgy but I didn't make a big deal out of it. I didn't say: 'My family will cut your legs off if you don't …' I never threatened people like that.

But my life was chalk and cheese. And Dad remained a phantom figure. When he did call in October 1980, over a year since I'd last heard from him, it was with a shock. Fanny had given birth to their daughter. I had a half-sister, Anna Marie. He gently told me how much he loved me and said he would call me in another couple of days

When he called next, nearly a year later, it was to tell me I had a half-brother, Emilio. Because he was known as Count Marco, Dad made out in the paperwork that Fanny's kids were my grandpa's children so they could have the Di Giovine name. Just like me.

He told me he thought of me every day and said, 'I promise I will see you as soon as I can.'

Understandably, Mum would fly into a rage after the phone calls. I was upset. I didn't even know where he was calling from and she'd quell her own fears by expressing them.

'You don't need to see him. Forget about him. He's upsetting you and he's not even here! He's not part of *our* life. Don't let him inside your head.'

Of course, Dad was well and truly there, superglued in. I so wanted to see him and be with him. Yet my body was sending my thoughts in all sorts of directions. In February 1983 a new and welcome complication came into my life when I found my first love, my puppy love. A lovely lad.

Michael Mason looked right out of Duran Duran. He was gorgeous. He was John Taylor's double, tall and a couple of years older than me. I really loved him. His sister was only five years old and we used to babysit for her together, so I got to know his family.

He'd been going out with one of my friends but he finished with her. I went to the amusement arcade his dad owned in Thornton-Cleveleys in Lancashire and he was there and asked me out. I knew my friend was still madly in love with him, so I decided I couldn't accept. It wouldn't be fair. I went to her and told her what had happened, because I knew she'd be hurt if she found out from someone else, but I assured her I wouldn't go out with him even though I liked him a lot.

She reacted with fury, insisting, 'You're not going out with him,' even though I'd told her I wouldn't, and calling me names. She was a big girl, quite forceful, and she'd just got done for grievous bodily harm. You wouldn't mess with her. But I was cross because I'd been honest with her and she still kicked off, so I thought, 'I'm not having that. I'm not having her tell me what to do.'

Michael asked me out again, and this time I said 'Yes'. She found out and it was all hell let loose. She stopped me in the playground at breaktime and accused me: 'You're going out with him.'

I just looked at her and said, 'Oh, fuck off.'

I turned, and she grabbed me by the back of my head and pulled me backwards. I stood my ground and gave as good as I got, but she was a tough girl. A teacher came, a little short man – we were taller than him – and broke us up.

What I'd done was bad, because she loved him and she had gone out with him first. You don't really do that to your friends. But I was stubborn and I didn't like the way she was behaving. She was a bully. A lot of the girls were scared of her so they all fell out with me. I became an outcast. They wouldn't dare come up to me and say to my face, 'Oh you bitch, you shouldn't have done that,' because they knew that I wouldn't stand for that. But they wouldn't speak to me.

One girl who did speak to me was Dawn, who was nice-looking and quite shy. I called her 'my shadow'. I was always the leader. It was just Dawn and me for a long time. At school we did our own thing but we had friends from other schools and from the area. I've never, ever found it hard to make friends.

Outside school it was Michael and me. I thought it was amazing going out with a boy whose father owned an arcade on the Blackpool seafront. We didn't have to wait in queues or pay to go on the machines. When we babysat at weekends his mum and dad would let me stay in the spare room. We'd worked up to some heavy petting and just under a year after we first went out he sneaked into that room one night. It was exciting and didn't seem wrong to be doing it and I lost my virginity at the age of thirteen. It was painful and awkward but I didn't worry about that. It was first love. Young love.

Sleeping with Michael diverted my thoughts from Italy. Mum was always busy working, or nesting in the first home she had ever had to herself, the council house in Poulton-le-Fylde. It looked to her as if she'd escaped. She'd built a wall between us and much of the past and prayed it wouldn't be breached. She didn't have a clue Michael and I were having sex and was just happy I wasn't nagging her about going to see Nan or asking if Dad was going to turn up. She was more tranquil. I could see it in her face. It was more calm. But it was always aware.

We received the phone call that changed everything in June 1983. Dad had just been arrested in New York. Count Marco Carraciolo had jumped a red light in Manhattan. A patrol car stopped him and he was arrested. At the precinct he was processed and fingerprinted and told if he paid $500 he'd be bailed.

He made his phone call to Fanny and told her to get the money there fast. She sent her brother. But Emo took his time, didn't concern himself about it – a traffic violation, no big deal – allowing more chance for Count Marco's details to be scrutinised. Because of recent diplomatic incidents the New York cops were being wary about any arrested foreigners and paying a lot of attention to them. Count Marco was certainly Italian but the fingerprint records revealed his real name was Emilio Di Giovine and he'd committed a murder in Milan. All politeness towards Count Marco ended then and there.

Instead of paying bail and going home, Dad was sent to the correctional facility in New Jersey while, quickly, all the necessary extradition procedures were rubber-stamped. It was no contest. As he waited in jail, Dad could only hope that in the three years he'd been Count Marco Nan had fixed as many people as possible over the Mafoda killing.

Even so, his circumstances did not seem as complicated or threatening as those of another prisoner being held by the Americans: a mystery man who had been implicated in the death of Roberto Calvi. Calvi, who was dubbed 'God's banker' because of his close Vatican links, was found hanging under London's Blackfriars Bridge on 17 June 1982. The prisoner who talked to Dad about Calvi's supposed suicide was 'in transit'. He told Dad the inside story of that mysterious incident involving the man who used to be chairman of the Banco Ambrosiano, which had collapsed in 1982 in a huge political scandal involving billions of illegally exported *lire*. It turned out Calvi was involved in laundering drug money. There were assorted stories about his involvement with the Vatican Bank and several other influential organisations. It was widely believed that he had not killed himself but had been what the Italians call 'suicided'. They even have a word for it: *suicidoto*.

Dad has wisely stayed silent about what he knows about the ongoing murder mystery of God's banker, and the man he'd talked to remained in custody when Dad was put on a plane back to Italy, where he was to face the consequences of shooting down Mafoda. He was surprisingly relaxed about it.

It was going to be more of an ordeal for Mum.

And me.

It was going to change our lives.

CHAPTER SEVEN
THE GOOD LIFE

*'We are a small country, but dig two metres and
you are among the Romans.'*

ITALIAN ROCK STAR VINICIO CAPOSSELA, 2009

Count Marco Carraciolo was fast-tracked out of America. They moved Dad quicker than any extradition treaty had ever intended. When he arrived in Rome only a couple of weeks after being handcuffed in Manhattan the lawyers joked that the ink wasn't dry on the paperwork: 'His feet didn't touch the ground. Emilio Di Giovine was a most unwanted man.' But that was only in America.

The Italian authorities desperately wanted him. They had tall filing cabinets stacked with folders of crimes he was suspected of. But they had no doubt that he had shot dead Mafoda and that's what they went after him for: murder. America had extradited him, Rome wanted to eliminate him, lock him up and throw away the key.

It was then that Nan's years of behind-the-scenes work paid off: the depths of her corruption were limitless. Dad's trial was quick and he was convicted of murder. The appeal by Nan's legal team was instant. They reduced the charge to manslaughter and his case was considered again. It was all done with money. By the time he appeared on the manslaughter charge a lot of people had received a lot of Nan's money. And it was only because Dad was such a high-profile criminal that he got any jail time at all. He had to be seen to be being punished and was sentenced to seven years in Parma prison. There's no parole system as such in Italy but you get three months off for every year of sentence. A year in jail is nine months. It wasn't going to be hard labour. Inside the court it was like a carnival, with Dad hugging Nan and his brothers and sisters. Well he might – he'd got away with murder. Especially when the sentence was reduced on appeal to three years.

That outcome sent a message to all the other *Mafiosi* and through the rest of the international underworld that the Di Giovine family could do pretty much as they wanted. They were untouchable, three years in Parma nothing but a fleabite to Dad. It wasn't even as much of an irritation as that. It was like a health retreat where he had silk sheets and exotic specialised 'nursing care' from an extremely attentive nurse.

Mum's face was a freeze-frame of anxiety when she took the phone call from Nan to tell her Dad was in prison in Italy. She couldn't have cared less where he was as long as he was out of our lives or, more importantly, my life. But this was the phone call Mum had never wanted, had been dreading. Dad wanted to see 'his little princess'.

It had never been possible before, for in America he had been someone else. It would have been too risky. Now there was nothing to stop him seeing me. Mum's face as she took the call was a mixture of fear and resignation. She was in the middle. She'd made a new life for us, built that wall around a castle for just the two of us. Not for a family of three.

Yet Dad wanted to see me. And I was desperate to see him.

I knew it was Nan on the phone and thought something bad had happened. Mum sat me down and told me he was in jail for some petty thieving and he wanted me to go over to Milan and see him but, she said, 'Marisa, you don't have to go. No one can force you if you say you don't want to. If you say you are too frightened to go into a prison I will tell Nan so that she can tell your father.'

I could tell she was longing for me to invent an excuse, but we both knew there was no way of disobeying Nan. It was like a royal command. And I wanted to go. Oh, so very, very badly. I was missing my nan, missing my family. I missed the culture, the lifestyle. Also, I could get away with stuff there as she wasn't nearly as strict as my mum.

Mum resigned herself to it. She had to. She put on a brave face but she wasn't taking any nonsense. She wanted to get over, see Dad and get back to Lancashire where she felt safe and secure. It didn't take long. We went in August 1983, not many weeks after Dad drove through that red Manhattan traffic light.

'Marisa! Get a move on!' Mum was nervous about the trip. She was hurrying me up and her accent became more and more Blackpool as the kitchen clock ticked on. 'Marisa! For the last time ...' On school mornings her voice used to sound like Kellogg's Rice Krispies – it would snap, crackle and then finally pop with frustration as she tried to get me out the house in time for my first class.

Today she was even more agitated. I was running late, listening to Duran Duran, doing my hair, worrying if I'd put on the right top. Did the shoes match? I wanted to look good. I was thirteen years old.

The taxi was waiting. From the bedroom window I could see the driver having a cigarette and reading the local weekly paper. He didn't know about my big news, that I was going to see my dad.

'*Marisa!*'

Mum was way over the top; the car was thirty minutes early, so there was no panic. Yet she was a bag of nerves. She'd been packed for a week. I couldn't be upset with her. It was a big day for her too. One she had feared. She'd been expecting it for a long time but that didn't make it any better.

After a twenty-four-hour train trip from Manchester, Uncle Franco was there to meet us at Milan Central Station and take us to Nan's. It was all hugs and kisses and shouting and chaos in the apartment, just like old times. Out rolled the familiar Fiat 500 cigarette-run car: Nan had enlisted a confidante to drive us to Parma prison.

I'd tossed around in bed all night and couldn't get my eyes to stay closed, but when it was time to get up I just wanted to sleep. I was bewildered by everything that was happening. It was like being in a dream, a hallucination. Whatever it was, I didn't want to wake up from it.

I'd no idea what to expect. We left early for Nan had some stops to make on the way from her apartment. As we went, she did a gourmet shop – lobster, fillet steak, fresh eggs and bread, soft and hard cheeses, a couple of hams, coffee beans, bottles of red and white wine, San Pellegrino water. She packed the car with expensive delicacies, chunks of cake and *amaretti* biscuits. It looked as though we were going to have a feast of a picnic.

I felt intimidated when I saw the prison with its huge grey walls, iron gates and tiny, barred windows. And I assumed there would be a long wait before I saw Dad because there was a line of people waiting for their visit. But Nan brushed breezily past them all as guards stopped searching other visitors to acknowledge her. She never dropped her pace till the last moment, when she smiled at someone and slipped a thick bundle into his pocket. He indicated the way to the visitors' room, which had a central marble table with benches on either side. Families were on one side and then the inmates began to file in. They all wore blue dungarees and white trainers, prison clones.

'How will I know my dad?' I asked Mum.

Nan laughed. 'Marisa, you'll see your papa in a minute, don't worry.'

And I did. He strode into the room, chatting casually to one of the guards. He was immaculate in a bespoke blue suit, white shirt and black shoes with a shine you could see your face in. His hair was salon neat, styled and gelled. He looked as though he'd stepped from a movie screen.

As he approached our table, he ignored Nan and Mum and lifted me high into his arms then pulled me close. I put my arms around his neck and held on tight. I saw tears appear in the corner of his eyes as he whispered in my ear: '*Spiacente* [sorry].'

He put me down and I held his hand across the table, unable to take my eyes off him.

'Marisa, I love you so much. I have missed you more than anyone else. I will be out soon and I dearly want to see you. Things will be different in the future. I will see to it.'

All the disappointments I'd suffered vanished as he spoke quietly to me. I was in heaven again.

He took the food and wine from Nan, part of his supplies, then they talked business and I knew not to listen. I'd already learned discretion; there are some things you are born with.

Mum clearly wasn't happy about the situation. She was happy for me but not for what this meeting would mean for the future. I could hardly look at her because I was so happy and I knew she wasn't. It didn't seem fair. I wanted all of us to be smiling and happy and hugging. Mum did her best but I could tell she was broken-hearted. In contrast, Dad seemed so pleased to see me, to compensate for all the years we'd missed together. He saw some spark in me that delighted him. He held onto me when the guards came to end the visit. Everyone else left and I was still holding his hand. Finally, he let go of me and leaned over and kissed me on the forehead, then he was off, talking to the guard who was helping him carry his gourmet packages.

It was a quiet journey back to Nan's. I wanted to make plans for the next visit but was clever enough to keep quiet.

Mum didn't know what to say. Nan, as always, knew what was going to happen but kept it to herself.

In Milan, Nan took me to the markets. It was a little bit of blackmail for she bought me anything and everything. Mum just watched; she wasn't in a shopping mood. She protested when Nan gave her gifts but Nan waved a finger at her: 'Patti! You never, ever refuse a gift from the family.'

Mum's face looked strange. It seemed to roll up, as if it was giving a shrug. What could she say to that?

We didn't talk much about what was on both our minds as we travelled back to – was it home? – Blackpool. At times on the trip Mum would grab me by the hand and pull me along a little bit as if, maybe, she was trying to shake sense into me. Her sense of the situation.

Later, back in England and on the train to Preston, she looked at me and said quietly: 'He's no good, Marisa. You don't need him. I know it's hard but don't be drawn in by this. Your life is in Blackpool with me, with your family, with your friends. Never, ever forget that.'

I already had when Dad picked me up in his arms in an Italian prison where he was serving time for shooting a man dead (although I still didn't know that's why he was there).

When we got back to Poulton all I wanted to do was return to Italy, to Parma to see my dad. Instead, it was back to school where everyone was talking about their school holidays, hiking in the Lake District, beaches in Spain, Bacardi and boys, suntans and sunburns. When I talked thirteen to the dozen to my best mates about visiting Dad in jail they looked confused. And how could they have understood?

It was hard enough for me. Especially with Mum. Every time I mentioned visiting again she would go into a wobbly: 'Why do you want to go back? Your school is here, your friends are here, I'm here. Why do you want to give up everything? Don't any of us count any more?'

After all she had gone through, all she had done for me, she felt betrayed. She'd brought me up to show respect for life and everyone around me. Now I wanted to go and visit a man in jail. But her own maternal instincts would not allow her to hurt me by bursting my bubble of beliefs about Dad. She said he was no good but didn't tell the thirteen-year-old me that he was in jail for killing a man and he was a drug smuggler. A major *Mafiosi*. I don't even know if that would have made a difference to how I felt. So I kept saving the money I was making working a Saturday job at a café. I kept it in a shoebox on the top of my wardrobe, where Mum found it. She knew what I was doing. It helped pay for our Italian summers. Well, it helped us to get there. If we thought we were the poor relations before, we were the poverty-stricken ones now.

The family was rolling in cash. Nan had gone into the real-estate business. She'd bought a bigger apartment in Via Christina Belgioso, close to Quarto Oggiaro. One auntie had another place, and another and another. The Di Giovine family dominated the square, spreading their domestic lives over ten apartments.

Nan, of course, held onto the original Piazza Prealpi apartment for old time's sake. Or bloody-mindedness. It was a council flat and she paid rent on it. It shouldn't have been allowed as she owned other property but the council wouldn't dare give it to someone else even if they knew it was vacant. It would just get burned down. Or the lives of the family who moved in would be made hell.

The family wealth didn't change their attitude or the general feelings towards them. It never stopped the fear of the family, which Nan promoted in her utter belief that it brought respect. The family had to get violent at times because of the reputation they'd built. People knew if you messed with one, you messed with all of them, so few ever tried. Those that did never came back to do it again.

It did change things for me and Mum: no more day-long train trips to Italy because in 1984 Nan started booking flights for us and arranging the car to meet us. When the morning came for the taxi to take us to Manchester airport I was packed and waiting at the front door before Mum's alarm clock jangled.

In Milan, Mum was open-eyed, astonished, at how well the family was doing. Uncle Franco collected us in a brand new BMW to take us to Nan's. The first thing Nan did was take us both shopping. We had so much stuff, dresses and shoes and the rest, we had to buy extra luggage to carry it all home. I was given money and clothes. A lot of them were my Auntie Angela's. She used to hate me coming because Nan would give me all her clothes. She and I were like sisters: we'd fight and scream at each other but we always looked out for each other as well.

Nan wanted me looking my best for my second prison visit to Dad. It was like Sunday best for church. The night before, I was so excited I couldn't sleep. I kept thinking it was a dream. Mum was beside me and she was also wide awake. My dream was her nightmare.

We were on parade early, and it was like a military operation. Nan, of course, was the General. We set off at 6 a.m. for the 75-minute drive from Milan to Parma prison. Nan used an old guy, a trusted family friend, as our taxi driver. She paid his petrol, liked his company. He smiled a lot at me. And carried two pistols, one strapped to his ankle.

Nan used to stop off at every single speciality shop and go direct to the top-end farms to pick up the best for Dad. He would create menus from the delivered produce, telling the prison chef what to cook for him each week. He ate better than the politicians in Rome.

Nan took him clean sheets, clean clothes, new clothes. He was living like a Roman emperor, his every wish a command. Every weekend he was invited to go and have a slap-up meal at a politician's house. At the first dinner the politician's wife asked who their guest was and Dad was described as the politician's new 'executive assistant'.

The five-star hotel treatment suited him. He felt stronger when he pulled me up in arms. He seemed to have put on weight but his grey designer suit still hung sleekly on him. The guards had cordoned off an area of the visiting room and we walked around. When we sat he gave me a silver bracelet. While the other visitors were hustled out, we were left alone.

Dad's VIP treatment, the big-screen telly in his cell, the showers when he wanted them, were all in return for Nan's payoffs. The prison guards' families received regular goodies, all manner of stolen gear, and it was always apparent who wanted drugs. Dad made sure there was no trouble in the prison. Everybody was happy. Especially me.

On the Italian visits we would always go down to Calabria, so there was sun and the seaside too. It was a ten-hour drive but it was fun because Auntie Angela was with me as well as various other family teenagers, cousins, aunts and uncles, and my Uncle Filippo's girlfriend Alessandra.

Mum was sort of in charge of us, along with Auntie Milina, but Auntie Milina never let us out. We'd have to be escorted, we couldn't go out on our own. Because we came from Milan, from the North, we were a novelty and all the lads there were desperate to be around us. I was tall and blonde and they were like flies buzzing round. We loved it. But when we gave our surname they'd run a mile. Or most of them would.

It was the brave ones who stayed. And they got slapped for talking to us. We didn't think it was fair. We wanted to go for a walk, to meet some of the local lads, but it didn't happen. We were housebound except when we were being chaperoned to the beach and back. We got fed up with Auntie Milina.

One day when she wouldn't let us out, Alessandra held a séance with a wooden ouija board. We all sat with our fingers on the glass and suddenly it started going really fast.

Alessandra said, 'Do something to Milina. Who is it? Who is it? Do something to Milina.'

Next thing, the glass spelled 'death'.

'No. No. No. Don't do that.' We were just young girls and we were terrified by this.

That same night there was an almighty thunderstorm. When we got up the next day and went down, Milina's arm was in a bandage. We all wanted to know what had happened to her and she told us: 'The windows and shutters flew open with the storm. I went to close them and I don't know what happened, but I stumbled out of the window onto the balcony.'

We were astonished. The balcony had just been built. A few weeks before it hadn't been there and she would have stumbled not onto the balcony but to her death. She was lucky, but it felt like an omen.

It was a scare but it didn't spoil the fun, and Mum was enjoying herself. Being a camera freak she took lots of photographs and in a fit of defiance we all posed topless. It was a huge joke and all of us are laughing in the pictures. It was a prank, a delight for us giggly girls, because all the relatives were so old-fashioned in Calabria compared to Milan. You couldn't even go out on a date alone. You had to take a chaperone. You weren't allowed to have a boyfriend.

One day I went to visit an old grandma while I was wearing a sun top. It was a very dry heat and in the summer it can get up to 40 degrees Celsius.

She said: 'You're not going out like that, are you?'

I said: 'I'm going to the beach!'

She said: 'You should cover your shoulders.'

I went off to the beach smiling. I was witnessing two different worlds, yesterday and today, in Italy. Mum and I spent six weeks there every summer and I absolutely loved it. I really wished I could live there. I hated coming back to a windy, cold, rainy Blackpool coast. I hated it. Of course, we always came back in September and straight into the cold and the gloom. That made it worse.

Yet I was young enough to get on with my life. I was well over first love Michael – we didn't split up, but before my fifteenth birthday we had drifted apart and gone our separate ways. I had a laugh, I had a lot of friends. But all the same ...

Mum had the history to support her constant argument: 'It's no good for you over there. I know that better than anyone. Forget about it.'

I couldn't.

In the summer of 1985, when I was fifteen, my school friend Dawn came along with Mum and me. We stayed at Nan's, and Dawn saw that life was fast and furious and she loved it. She saw the luxury and the money. Uncle Antonio, who had created his own empire, had an absolutely sensational penthouse in Nan's block. He'd bought two apartments and knocked them through, and he also had a villa by the Lakes where we used to go.

One day he decided to take Dawn and me to Rimini. It was the usual summer nightmare on the roads with massive queues. Uncle Antonio steered his Maserati onto the hard shoulder and drove almost all the way to Rimini speeding past the blocked lines of cars. It was like an oven outside, but we had the radio and the air-conditioning full on, speeding along in this Maserati. Dawn and I felt like royalty – especially when we took a suite at the Grand Hotel in Rimini.

Uncle Antonio was a huge cocaine fiend and he travelled with suitcases of cocaine. We went out to long lunches and lived the high life. My Auntie Domenica, known to all as 'Mima', who'd joined us for the trip, was ten years older and more sophisticated than us. She'd looked like a bloke – a strong face, if I'm being kind – before the nose operation that she had while Dad was in New York. Now she was quite startling-looking, and she took a liking to some of the younger men. Though not quite as much as the liking she had taken to heroin.

She wasn't the only junkie I knew, not by any means. Sadly, Uncle Filippo's girlfriend Alessandra had a problem with that as well. Tallish for an Italian girl, beautiful and vibrant, she was only a couple of years older than me, and I was deeply shocked by what happened to her. It was a warning bell, if any of us had cared to listen.

CHAPTER EIGHT
ROMEO

*'Whatever happens to you has been waiting
to happen since the beginning of time.'*

MARCUS AURELIUS, AD 172

It was as if the ouija board was sending another message, for the family fortunes suffered a severe knocking in 1986.

It kicked off with Nan's arrest. It made sense to the police not on the payroll. Milan was turning into a suburb of Colombia, there was so much drug traffic. The cops believed Dad was no longer a problem as he was in jail. So they took Nan off the streets on a drug handling and stolen goods list of charges. They couldn't prove much but she was sent to San Vittore prison for two years.

I was heartbroken. Nan had been my guardian angel, had organised everything, and now she was in jail. I thought I would never see Dad or the rest of the family again.

Then I heard that Alessandra had died, and I felt everything around me was crumbling. She'd taken a drug consignment to America for the family. She was a mule; all she had to do was deliver the package. It's still a mystery exactly what happened to her. What we know is that she overdosed on heroin and whoever she was with bundled her out of a speeding car and into a Manhattan side street. She was thrown into the trash and left to die. We don't know who she was with, what she was doing or why it happened. But that's what the cops said she died of.

Of course, she was seen as a minor casualty in a billion-dollar business. Uncle Filippo was devastated, as were her family. My uncle tried to find out what actually happened but there wasn't much of a result. If it had been a family member it would have been different. I know that sounds awful but because it was his girlfriend, not family, the odds of business against vendetta came down on the side of business. It's brutal, but that was the way of it. When I heard the news I was horribly sad, and it felt freaky thinking about the strange night with the ouija board when she'd sent Auntie Milina the death message. Had it backfired?

Drugs were taking their toll on the family. Dad's lesbian sister Mariella, who'd had the affair with his girlfriend, had become a serious heroin user and became infected by a dirty needle. She contracted HIV and died from full-blown AIDS. But it didn't stop business.

With Nan imprisoned, Dad quickly got on with the job of setting up new operational headquarters. He was open all hours inside the all-mod-cons Parma Hospital. He rein-vented his scam from Barcelona with a series of clever twists: instead of working in the prison hospital to case it out, he was living in the nearby regular hospital in grand style. A doctor had ordered Dad to have twenty-four-hour care as he claimed he risked dying of an infection from lead left in the gunshot wounds he suffered in the café attack when Adele was killed. There were no guards, only the consultant, chain-smoking tax-free cigarettes, who'd been enriched in return for the dodgy paperwork to get Dad into hospital. When the prison authorities asked how long it might take for him to get better, the consultant said he could give no time limit.

Dad ran everything from there, organising the family's affairs – and his own – like a free man. Sometimes contacts and my uncles would visit four or five times a day with meetings going until late in the evening. Information was received and orders given about the international drug shipments. Every night someone from the family, usually Auntie Rita, would drive out to Parma and make deliveries to Dad and hand out any necessary payoffs. They'd go over the accounts, the drugs sold and money made. Given the enormity of the deals, maybe it was appropriate that Dad wore a blue business suit for his hospital board meetings. But it was crazy. He was in hospital because he was meant to be near death from lead poisoning and he wasn't even in pyjamas.

Sex was Dad's recreational drug. He was enraptured by one of the nurses and he engaged in quite a passionate affair for a man in critical condition. Nurse Leggy – yes, she had long legs – and her husband couldn't have children but she got pregnant by Dad. Her marriage survived, with her pretending the boy was her husband's. Nurse Leggy thought enough of Dad to send him a photograph of the baby, who they named Alessandro, and tell him: 'This is your son.'

So I've got a half brother I've never seen who doesn't know who we are. But there are probably more; one thing

Dad never struggled to do was attract the eye of women. Sometimes he'd happily see double.

I was seeing red. I was angry at I don't know what. My situation, my circumstances – at Mum?

I did pretty well at school despite the usual distractions, the crushes and the fashion moments, and decided on a college degree in business studies, which was as much for Mum as for me. But my mind wandered from management and economics to what was happening with Dad and Nan and the rest of the family in Milan. I'd seen the glamour and excitement, I'd been part of it. Now I wasn't.

My seventeen-year-old's moods and 'it's not fair' attitude didn't help my relationship with Mum. She was doing everything she could to keep a good and happy home – in England. And I was going on about the family in Italy. I wouldn't call them all screaming matches but we had many exchanges of opinion. Our lives were very difficult. Every seventeen-year-old knows she's right. Every Mum knows she's right. It's a Mexican stand-off that neither can win.

When the 1987 Easter break arrived I'd done six months of college and what seemed like a century of mum-and-daughter disputes. We were both at our wits' end when I called Auntie Angela in Milan to get the latest news and gossip. Auntie Rita answered the phone and everything poured out of me – the frustration, the boring life in England, the wanting to see Dad, all of it.

She got the message: 'Marisa, come here! Stay with me. You can see your dad every day.'

I had college holidays, money saved, and Mum didn't have the energy to fight me about it. It was agreed I'd only go for a month until it was time to come back for college. Mum was fine, helping me get organised for the trip, helping me pack, but for all that her face told another story – one of resignation. Like mother, like daughter. Life was repeating itself in front of her eyes.

I hadn't seen my family in more than a year and never without Nan. Uncle Guglielmo, who met me at the airport, was the outside organiser for Dad, who was masterminding everything from his hospital rooms. Just because Nan and Dad were in jail didn't mean they weren't still running one of the biggest drug rings in Europe with the USA their biggest customer.

I was desperate to see Dad again and Uncle Guglielmo arranged for me to have a driver, a young guy called Bruno, for my trips to the hospital. I didn't pay much attention to him at first. I saw him give me the eye, the up and down look. I was young with a good figure and long blonde hair so it wasn't the first time I'd been ogled. Hey, I'd have been upset if he hadn't!

But it was Dad's attention I really wanted. It was as if he was in a corporate office; he had his own airy, private ward with nice big windows on the second floor of the hospital. I spent the day with him and the next and the next.

'I'm sorry I wasn't around so much for you when you were growing up,' he said. 'But soon I'll be out and things will change. Things will be better. I want you here as much as you can be. I want you around more.'

I'd no real idea of the scope of what Dad and Nan and the family were involved in but I wasn't stupid either. My father and grandmother were in jail, most of my uncles had been in jail, so I was aware they weren't running Disney World. I knew their business must be dodgy but I didn't ask questions. I was just happy to be there, to be *home*. For that's how it felt. I feel Italian, I always have. When I was seventeen I just wanted to stay.

I spent most days with Dad but there were regular interruptions with his constant stream of visitors. Whenever he spoke to people they listened to his words as if their lives depended on it. And there was no better example of that than Bruno. I could see Dad liked him and they would often spend time alone talking about business. On the first visit they finished their conversation by shaking hands and as we left Dad kissed me and shouted to Bruno: 'Don't fuck it up, Bruno. And make sure you look after my princess.'

Bruno did, but more than Dad imagined or wanted.

I found myself warming to Bruno more and more. He was a good-looking, big strong guy with nice brown eyes. He was four years older than me and wore decent clothes, designer jeans and shirts, sharp suits and cap-toed leather brogues. He looked good, he looked successful and he was trusted by my dad. What wasn't there to like?

He was also fun. In the car he would do silly things, pull faces or tell me jokes and make me laugh. I was young and giggly and he was confident and he knew how to press the right buttons to amuse and impress a seventeen-year-old girl. The problem – there's always one – was that he was impressing lots and lots of girls. All the girls who used to come and go from the apartment fancied him. He had an on-off relationship with my cousin Magda, who was my Auntie Santina's daughter from a previous marriage. I say on-off but for Bruno it was basically off except that Magda did everything for him. She would run around asking him if he wanted anything to eat and do his washing and he mostly ignored her. She was totally smitten but I thought he was a jerk the way he treated her.

Bruno's parents owned a bakery in Milan which supplied food on contract to schools. It was a steady and financially rewarding business. His folks wanted him to work with them but Bruno was too independent in his attitude. He liked life working for Dad. Which gave him every opportunity for drinking with my uncles and indulging in the free-flowing cocaine always on call.

He spent more time at the apartment than at his parents'. We girls would sit around in the evening watching videos when most of the men were out on the town. Bruno stayed with us one night and we all watched *Scarface*. Bruno started imitating Al Pacino as the cocaine-crazy Tony Montana waving his machine gun, 'my little friend', in the air. I thought he was being really stupid, but Magda and the other girls were in hysterics.

Suddenly Bruno called out to me: 'Hey, Marisa! This guy is just like your daddy.'

He was pointing at Al Pacino blasting people to bits on the screen. I must have looked puzzled for he quickly said, 'No, no, beautiful. I'm only joking.'

Bruno realised I didn't know as much as he'd thought about Dad's empire. Before visiting Dad the next day he took me for a spin on his Vespa. We sped around the streets and he was joking with people we passed.

'You've dropped some money back there,' he yelled, and they'd walk half a mile back to look for this imaginary money. It was silly things like that as a seventeen-year-old I thought were hilarious. He was always laughing and fun. He was a nice guy. And he was good-looking. I found myself looking him up and down.

Dad instantly saw there was a spark between me and Bruno and didn't waste his breath. 'Bruno, if you've been playing around with my princess I'll cut your cock off.'

I couldn't believe what I was hearing.

Bruno nearly fell off his chair.

'Emilio! You've got it all wrong. You think I would be that stupid?'

Bruno *was* that stupid. And I loved him for it. But there would be no romance for a while. He was a close friend of my Uncle Guglielmo and together they were running the family business on the outside. Huge drug shipments were arriving at Gioia Tauro and being trucked to Milan, where they had to be processed. Organising the distribution involved team work and the family had a workforce numbering sixty – guys of Bruno's age who had earned

Nan and Dad's trust and who had been vouched for by them.

Blood family and non-kin membership of the 'Ndrangheta overlap. Marriages like Nan and Grandpa Rosario's help smooth relations within each *'ndrina* and expand membership. At the bottom of the chain of command are the *picciotti d'onore* [soldiers], who are expected to perform tasks with blind obedience until they are promoted to the next level of *cammorista*. That's when they're given command over their own soldiers. The secret of the power and success of the 'Ndrangheta is that only an inner circle of relatives and trusted commanders have the core knowledge of all the operations of the family.

Bruno, at only twenty-one years old, was a *cammorista*. He was one of the few of their operators Uncle Guglielmo and Dad trusted to listen and understand what had to be done in the drug trafficking and make sure people did it. He'd be told precisely when and where shipments were coming in, the amount and where it needed to go. And Bruno only needed to be told once. Dad never liked to say anything twice.

But Dad didn't mind doubling up with girls, especially when they were as stunning as Mara and Marina. The twins. They were identical. Even in their heroin habits. They were both in Parma Hospital's drug rehabilitation centre. They had blonde hair, blue eyes and were slim, very sunny-looking and attractive women. They wore funky clothes and were spoiled rotten by their parents, who had plenty of money, a very rich Parma family. Their parents would have paid anything to get them clean.

Dad's interest in the twins wasn't purely for pleasure. He knew he couldn't stay in the hospital for ever. He knew he had to go back inside at some point. He had to make other arrangements. He hooked up with Marina, who was a bit of a devil. He told her that if her parents invested some money, they could open a bakery partnership. He told her to tell her father it would be good rehab therapy. It worked, and when Dad went back to prison he started working in the bakery on day release and going back to his luxury cell at night.

It was his own business, but it was in the twins' name. He needed to keep them sweet. But they fell out because Dad started liking the other twin, Mara. The *ménage à trois* didn't quite work. The bakery did, though, allowing Dad all the freedom and time he needed.

I was due back at college. I didn't want to go. I wanted to stay, with Dad, with Bruno. Mum was going crazy back in England. She was on the phone all the time demanding to know what plane I'd be on. I avoided the question, stuck my head in the sand about all of that. Bruno was foremost in my mind almost all the time.

One night after we got back from visiting Dad I saw the other side of Bruno, the brutal *Mafiosi* part of him. We'd gone to our regular disco in Milan with Magda and her mates. As I was standing at the side of the dance floor, a lad came up and asked me where the toilets were. I pointed to them but before he could move, Uncle Guglielmo, who I hadn't known was there, appeared, mad-eyed with cocaine. He hammered the lad in the face, battering him with punch after punch until the guy's nose was spread across his face and blood was pouring from his mouth. When he fell to the ground my uncle started kicking him while everyone watched.

Bruno appeared and joined in, kicking the guy even when he was out of it, out cold. They kicked him so hard they both bust their shoes. I'd never seen anything like it. They thought he was chatting me up – 'Hi, gorgeous', that sort of line – and they'd all but killed him for it.

When I told them what the lad had really said, Uncle Guglielmo grunted, 'He shouldn't have spoken to you.'

Back at the apartment, still upset about what I had seen, I asked about it again. Uncle Guglielmo was more reasonable without the cocaine and he put his arms around me and said, 'Marisa, all you need to know is your family will always protect you. Nobody fucks with us. That's all you need to know.'

In the circumstances, I shut up and concentrated on having a good time with Bruno. He took me shopping and out for lunch. We drove to Lake Como and went to Rome to see all the sights, the ancient Roman history, and it was romantic. And innocent. I realised loads of girls fancied him but he wanted to spend time with me, and that made me feel special.

But I had to return to Mum. He drove me to the airport and before I went through passport control he kissed me on the lips. Our first kiss. It was only a peck but it felt amazing. He put his arms around me and said, '*Ciao, bella.*'

I cried my heart out all the way back to Manchester. I was so distressed the stewardess sat next to me to make sure I was OK, and that I wasn't going to jump out at 35,000 feet.

When I got home I walked straight past Mum and started writing Bruno a letter.

I was shaky. I felt my life depended on knowing when I was going to see him again. I don't know if I was seduced by Bruno or by a combination of Bruno and my whole life experience in Italy. My mind, like my genes, was divided. I had a weird choice between gloom and doom. In my heart, inside me, I knew Bruno could and would protect me from anything. And I wanted a strong man to care for me.

But Bruno needed looking after too. A drug exchange in Milan had gone wrong and Bruno had to get out of town until the cops could be straightened.

Uncle Guglielmo told him: 'Go, lose yourself.'

So a month after I'd left Italy he rang me from Manchester Airport asking for directions to Blackpool. I was ecstatic. He'd just got on a plane, along with his mate Coby, the sixteen-year-old son of Uncle Guglielmo's girlfriend. Coby had brought loads of cash, more than £1,000, and his girlfriend Sarah. Bruno had bags and bags of marijuana. He'd thought nothing of bringing it through customs. That was what he did for a living, smuggled dope.

They hired a car and after Bruno figured out driving – at high speed – on the left-hand side of the road, they arrived on my doorstep. We took two rooms at a bed and breakfast in Blackpool. I forgot all about college classes and going home to Mum.

Mum wasn't very happy. I was. This was the excitement I'd been craving, with no boring spreadsheets and business charts and graphs. This was real life, another taste of the pace, intrigue and excitement of Milan. It was also sex, drugs and Duran Duran. Bruno and Coby used the marijuana as though they were sending smoke signals. They were puffing constantly. As we walked along Blackpool Pier or on the pleasure beach. They didn't care.

At first I only smoked joints with them in our rooms so as not to look like some innocent kid, but soon I got into enjoying it. It was relaxing and, along with the booze we were putting away, let my troubles drift away.

Driving around with Bruno made me feel all grown up, part of a team. We were a partnership. I liked that. And Bruno was cute and gentle when he did silly things. It made him more lovable. He wanted to be this macho man who could handle anything.

Especially cars. We stopped on the Fleetwood road to get some petrol and he filled up with diesel. We'd only gone a few hundred yards when we conked out. A white-haired driver stopped to help and worked it out immediately: 'You've put in the wrong stuff, mate!'

Bruno was aghast. He went bright red. He was so embarrassed. I gave him a huge hug and a kiss.

From then on he drove like a maniac, trying to show he was king of the road. Bruno loved cars and so did I. I knew all about them because I'd grown up around men who drove the best. I loved the speed and wind in your hair, the thrill of it. But speeding about is not a good idea around Blackpool with its irritating thirty-mile-an-hour limits everywhere, and we were stopped. Luckily we weren't hurtling around the place, but Bruno was pushing his luck. The copper was good about it. He studied Bruno's Italian licence, asked how long he was staying and then looked straight at me. Did he know Bruno was wanted in Milan? That was silly – how could he? But what was it?

It turned out he was Blackpool's laughing policeman: 'Tell your man this is not Monza.'

We were on our way with a ticking off. Bruno shrugged it off. I was relieved, and I'd liked the sound of 'your man'.

One morning at the B&B I woke up and saw a huge concrete flower tub in the room that should have been at the front of the building. Bruno had gone out drinking with a male friend of Dawn's and they'd got back drunk and brought it upstairs. They thought it was hilarious. The land-lady didn't.

We moved out and into a flat, and I slept with Bruno the first night there. I bled a little and he went 'Ooh', thinking he'd taken my virginity. He seemed pleased so I just went along with it. I never told him he wasn't actually the first. It was my first serious lovemaking and he was not a wham-bang-thank-you-ma'am merchant. He took care, and time.

Which I wasn't doing with Mum. She was going ballistic. I went home every couple of days or so to try and keep the peace and do some washing and collect clothes. I told her I was seeing people on holiday from Italy and, my mistake, said one of them was a friend of Dad's.

She asked more and I explained I'd met Bruno on my trip, he'd been the driver. She couldn't tolerate that. She was straight on the phone to Italy to Uncle Guglielmo. Who was this lad?

He said Bruno was a good guy, a safe guy. He was honest and told her that Bruno was avoiding the police and that he didn't know where he was and – no mobile phones – couldn't contact him.

Mum could. She found a note with the B&B name in some jeans I'd left for the wash. She screamed round to the place. We'd moved by then and she was greeted by our TV sitcom Blackpool landlady. They were two very unhappy and pissed-off ladies. We hadn't exactly been staying at the Ritz.

'Disgusting kids! They've gone, and they've left a right mess. There was even a pregnancy test in the bin.'

Pregnancy! Marisa! Italian boy! That was a hat-trick of horror for Mum. *Déjà vu.* A disaster.

When she confronted me I tried to explain. 'That pregnancy test wasn't mine. It was that girl Sarah's, who is with the other lad. Honestly, it wasn't mine. Mum, it's not mine.'

But she was back on the phone to Milan. By now that side of the family were in a rage at Bruno. And at me. They hadn't known where he was but they certainly hadn't expected him to be pleasuring himself – and me – in Blackpool. Dad was told, he had to be, and was furious. He wanted Bruno back in Italy, and by then Bruno had no choice.

The money had gone.

And so was he after I kissed him goodbye at Manchester Airport. I wasn't too upset. It was only a few weeks until the summer break and my annual trip to Milan. I said as much to Mum. She put me straight. In fact, she read the riot act.

'You vanished with this guy for nearly three weeks. What's wrong with you? Don't you care about anybody else? What has got into you? Everybody is angry, really angry. Forget about going, they won't let you back after this.'

I told her not to be silly. Nan loved me. Dad loved me.

It was a few days later when Uncle Guglielmo telephoned with some devastating news. Dad was ferociously upset about Bruno and me. He didn't want to see me.

Ever again.

My whole world fell apart.

CHAPTER NINE
STREET JUSTICE

'Tempt not a desperate man.'

WILLIAM SHAKESPEARE,
ROMEO AND JULIET

When he returned to the Piazza Prealpi, Bruno walked into slaps across the face from Uncle Guglielmo. The blows were physical and verbal and all stung.

'See Marisa, I'll rip your head off.

'See Marisa, Emilio will cut your balls off.

'See Marisa, you are a dead man.

'Get it? Understand?'

Bruno did, but if I needed any proof about how much he cared for me I got it when I returned to Milan that summer of 1987. I owed it all to Auntie Rita, who once again offered me a bed, somewhere to stay. She was erratic, and her amphetamine intake was frightening. There was no telling what she would do, how she would react. Yet she was my saviour.

There were some terrible scenes with Mum when I told her that I was going to Milan.

'You'll see that lad again and there'll be trouble. You wait and see. Just wait.'

But I was miserable living in Blackpool. I wasn't a child and I was so determined, so sure, that I had to go.

Uncle Guglielmo was waiting for me when I got to Auntie Rita's. He ignored any formalities and ranted at me. It went on for several minutes and the message was very loud and very clear: 'Stay away from Bruno.'

I asked how my dad was but he said not to bother asking as he was furious with me: 'Your father doesn't want you to be with this guy. He wants you to settle down, meet a lawyer, a doctor, someone else. Not Bruno.'

Although Bruno was a friend of the family and of my uncle, Dad didn't want me to be with him because he was who he was. The family had sorted out the prosecutors and Bruno was free to move around the city, as long as he stayed clear of me. It was a similar deal for me.

I cried myself to sleep at Auntie Rita's. I couldn't see the two most important men in my life. Bruno was forbidden. Dad had disowned me.

Despite the distress, I knew for sure that Bruno was my man. He said he'd rather be dead than not see me. That was over-the-top romantic but obviously there had to be some caution.

Auntie Rita suggested to Uncle Guglielmo that she and I needed a bit of space. Angela and the other girls could come around and she told her brother she would speak to me about Bruno and sort that out. Guglielmo agreed because he was run off his feet following Dad's instructions and watching his own back. Family informants had warned him he was under twenty-four-hour police watch.

With Uncle Guglielmo off the scene, Bruno became part of it again. He'd got himself a red Alfa Romeo Spider Series III and we'd howl off to Lake Como to a special spot we'd found and make love in the open air. Bruno was as crazy about me as I was about him. But I wanted to be with him all the time, not just for an hour here and there. I had to come to terms with the competing demands of business and the peccadilloes of the Milan man. Which Bruno followed to the letter. He would spend the day with me but on the stroke of 6 p.m. he was off drinking and gambling with his mates. Or going to San Siro to watch AC Milan – they were all football fanatics. I was jealous of him being away and especially being away and doing things I knew nothing about.

Auntie Rita, who eased her own concerns with her daily dose of amphetamines, read me some of the rule book: 'Get over it, honey. That's our life. Don't ask, for you don't need to know.'

But I did. At that time Bruno was on cocaine constantly. His parents had bought a brand new bakery van on the back of a state school contract. The day they got it Bruno got totally out of his head and took it for a drive with twenty of his mates on board. Twenty! He didn't get very far before he'd smashed it around a lamppost, mangled it into scrap. A couple of the guys had to go to hospital but Bruno jumped out and limped off.

His mum and dad, who never knew that he had nicked it, reported it as stolen. These people grafted; every penny they earned, they worked hard for by baking during the night. Bruno was mortified and never told them he'd nicked the van.

He was reckless, and had no respect for his family and how hard they worked, but I was blind to it. I was in love with him. He could do no wrong in my eyes. I felt he was just a bit wild. The kind of guy who likes a drink, who I knew was taking drugs and who would get into fights.

Yet before long I witnessed two displays of incredible violence, both teetering on the edge of murder. And I was the reason, possibly the excuse.

Rita suggested that Bruno and I come to a seaside caravan park on the outskirts of Rimini for a couple of days, along with her and her fourteen-year-old son Massimo. I thought it would be a chance for us to spend some proper time together away from *his* friends and possible trouble from *my* family, so we agreed.

As soon as we were settled in the caravan park, we went to the local fairground. We were having a great time on the rides when some guy came up to me and asked for a light for his cigarette. I said I couldn't help and he lost it: 'OK, then why don't you go and fuck off.'

Massimo stepped in, shouting, 'Why are you talking to her like that? Say sorry.'

The guy just laughed at Massimo, who was only a little lad, and walked away.

'I'm going to go and get Bruno,' shouted Massimo.

'No, please don't do that,' I begged. 'Bruno will go mad and we'll have to leave. Just don't say anything. It's not a big deal.'

I went to the toilets. Massimo looked like an ordinary kid but he was a tough little bugger and was already dealing drugs on the family's piazza. He wasn't going to let it go. He went to Bruno. When I reappeared a huge crowd had gathered by some steps. At the top was Bruno. He was bouncing this guy's head off the metal posts fixed to each of the stairs and shouting, 'Motherfucker. Motherfucker.'

The boy was screaming for him to stop but all he got in return was: 'Motherfucker, fucking motherfucker!' And his skull was bounced off another railing. Another, and another. I heard the thuds.

I thought Bruno was going to kill him.

Bruno thought he had killed him.

He was dead-eyed. I'd never seen that zoned-out look before. He'd blocked out the crowd around him and was hammering this guy again and again and again.

His victim finally blacked out and crumpled into a pool of blood.

Bruno ran out of the park, with Massimo and me chasing after him.

I screamed: 'You might have killed that guy!'

'I know. That's why we have to go. Now! We have to get out of here.'

When we got back to the caravan Bruno told Rita we had to get going. Rita, at thirty years of age, was a veteran of disorder and didn't need to ask why. We heard the screeching of the police and ambulance sirens but we drove off before we saw their flashing blue lights.

I should have been scared. I should have been terrified. I wasn't. The guy had been rude to me, and although he didn't deserve to get beaten up so badly I was proud Bruno wanted to defend me. I felt that with Bruno by my side no one could hurt me. I fell into his arms and went to sleep as we drove back to Milan. Where more trouble was waiting.

It was hot and humid that August and, as usual in that month, the streets were deserted. A couple of weeks later, Aunt Angela and I were on our way back from the Piazza Prealpi to Auntie Rita's. It was after 11 p.m. and the tram wasn't running. It's about a twenty-minute walk, no hassle on a warm night.

We got to within a few hundred yards of Auntie Rita's house when I was grabbed from behind. I thought it was my cousin Massimo fooling around – he was always trying to scare me.

'Get off her! Get off her,' I heard Angela screaming, and I turned. There was a ghostly man dressed in all white, white linen top and pants. He had this brown bag, like a satchel.

I shouted, 'Get off, you idiot. What are you doing?' I still didn't think it was anything to be too worried about. I thought the guy was stupid, not a killer.

A moment later I knew he was a lunatic. He thrust a long-bladed knife between my legs and growled, 'If you move, I'm going to cut you. I'll put this knife inside you. And cut you.'

He wasn't a particularly strong-looking guy but the knife was terrifying. I thought, 'My God, if he stabs that in down there I'll never have babies.'

But I had to keep calm. It happened in seconds, and Angela was rigid on the spot. It was all in freeze-frame.

The man in white pulled the knife to my neck. He got his cock out and started touching himself, demanding, '*Sega, sega* [Wank me off].'

I looked at him and asked, 'Do you know who I am?'

His eyes were gone. He was on something. We were caught at a blind spot on the road, nobody could see us. He could have done anything. He started looking around him.

Again, I asked, 'Do you know who I am?'

At that moment he let go and I yanked my arm back and ran out on to the road and legged it towards Auntie Rita's.

But Angela had already got there and Rita was on her way to help. She ran in the opposite direction with a giant carving knife, completely off her head on speed. If she had caught the man in white she would have stabbed him to death and probably not known anything about it.

By this time I was shaking and crying. I hadn't been like that in front of him because I knew I had to keep it together. The guy had taken off by the time Rita got to the spot.

But what did the dumb divvy do? He walked down to the Piazza Prealpi and bothered another girl on the way. There were some lads near her and the guy backed off. He got paranoid and went into the Motta Bar, across from my Nan's. These lads started ganging up outside. Then word got to them that I'd been attacked. They heard a description of the guy and knew it was him. They were all outside and wanting to kick his head in. They didn't go inside, though, out of respect for the bar owner, a woman who's a friend of my family. They didn't want to smash it up.

Uncle Filippo arrived and went straight in: 'What's going on, mate? What's happening?'

The bloke said: 'Don't know what's going on out there. I've done nothing wrong, but I daren't go out.'

'It's all right. Come out, come out, I'll help you. I'll sort it out, don't worry.'

Outside the bar, just as they were passing through the tables and chairs, Uncle Filippo started battering him.

'That was my niece you pulled the knife on. You want fun, do you?'

He kept hitting, a torrent of punches. The other lads piled in with the tables and chairs, smashing them into the guy and stabbing him with broken bottles. It went on for a long time. Blood was pouring from him, his white outfit soaked with red, when Bruno arrived.

Auntie Rita, racing around with carving knife in hand, had bumped into Bruno and told him what had happened. Someone else told him where to go. He looked at this guy who was already half dead, maybe three-quarters. He was certainly in some sort of coma, out cold.

Bruno stamped on his head. Then he rested his foot on this pervert's head and said: 'You're lucky. I'd have killed you.'

He spat in the guy's face and walked off.

Nobody had called the police. My family were the police. But the crowds and the noise invited them anyway. Nobody got done for the pervert's beating. What was the guy supposed to say? There were people in the bar but they 'didn't see anything'.

Horrible as it was, my attacker's battering gave me some sort of comfort. It was like having security. I felt nobody could get to me, could harm me. I was unbreakable. I was untouchable. I was my father's daughter and this was my family. And this is how they dealt with anyone who invaded their space or their people. They would go as far as was needed to protect you. I was part of that now, part of the Mafia.

No longer was I just thinking in Italian; I was thinking like an Italian *Mafiosi*. It's not indoctrination but day-to-day life that gives you a set of values that you soon find normal. It's like reciting the alphabet: after a time you don't have to think about it. You just *know* it.

I thought it was the pervert's bad luck that he went to the Piazza Prealpi. He probably didn't realise he was lucky to be alive. He was all broken apart but he was breathing. If my dad had got hold of him – my god!

Most girls would have been terrified, gone blank, not been able to say anything if they were grabbed in the street like that. Just done what he said. His eyes were glazed. He looked as if he'd escaped from a mental hospital.

He got his justice, though. Imagine if you did that to every pervert? They'd think again before abusing kids, abusing young girls. I wish it could be like that. My family could have got done for it, as could all the rest of the lads around the area, but that didn't stop them for a split second. That guy had invaded our restricted world.

But as far as Mum was concerned I'd overstayed my welcome in it. I was meant to be back at college in September but I was still in Milan and she was screaming down the phone: 'You're not eighteen yet. If you don't come now, I'll get you done.'

She was within her rights, and the Italian authorities would have backed her all the way. Of course, I now believed I was above all that. I was part of the clandestine clan. Untouchable. But I got an urgent lesson about that. We were not immune from the cops.

Rita had two children, Massimo and a daughter Elena. She had separated from their father and by September 1987 she had married Salvatore Morabito and they'd had a baby son Michael. Salvatore was from Calabria. One of Dad's cousins had told him to look us up in Milan, where he soon became part of the organisation and a regular courier to New York. He looked the part – respectable, no criminal record, a regular guy and a perfect heroin mule. Rita, sometimes with Nan, would collect him when he arrived back at Milan airport. They clicked after the third trip and became partners in life and drug dealing.

One night I was at their place watching television with Elena, in between playing on the couch with the baby, when there was a rap on the front door of the apartment. Auntie Rita came in from the bedroom and put her finger to her lips. She peered through the spyhole in the door and saw Salvatore almost filling the doorway. Then she saw the cops beside and behind him.

There was a back stair and she pointed at me and then at it: 'Marisa! Get out! Run, run!'

There wasn't time. The door was kicked in. I'd never seen so many cops in my life. There was a swarm of them.

Two fresh-faced officers marched over to me and put their hands on my shoulders: 'Sit down.'

I started to ask something.

'Quiet! Don't move.'

'But ... I ... what ...?'

'Quiet or we'll arrest you.'

I shut up.

When I looked over they had Auntie Rita and Salvatore handcuffed and banged up against the wall. The cops were tearing through the apartment, emptying drawers, looking inside cupboards, pulling up the carpet. They took each room in turn, double-checking and then checking again. They found scores of bags of heroin in the kitchen, hidden in soap-powder boxes beside the washing-up liquid, squeezy sponges and thin bleach underneath the sink.

They escorted Auntie Rita, Salvatore and the kids out of the apartment. They just left me there. On the couch. I stared at the TV, which was still on, showing a bizarre soap opera called *Licia Dolce Licia*.

I was mesmerised, but not by the TV antics of Manuel De Peppe. I couldn't think. Moments before I'd been bouncing a baby on my knee. I was hurt and angry – at myself as much as anything or anyone. Because I didn't understand. I'd thought the family was untouchable.

I went to Nan's and questioned Uncle Guglielmo. He couldn't understand my concern and was laughing: 'Marisa, quit worrying about it. None of this has anything to do with you. They didn't take you away because they know you are Emilio's daughter. They know you are not involved. It doesn't matter. This is life for us.'

And for me if I stayed in Milan with Bruno. Mum knew that and when she heard a whisper about the drugs raid and the arrests from one of my cousins she came to get me. She had to take the train – I was the one running around in high-powered cars and living well – as she couldn't afford the air fare. She demanded I come home with her there and then. I was screaming at her to let me stay. I didn't want to be bossed around by her but she had the ace argument: until I was eighteen I had to do as *she* said. I had no choice but to go back to Blackpool.

Mum was so determined to get me out of there she'd brought enough money to fly us both back to Manchester. I met Bruno before I left. We had no time to say more than goodbye.

I went with Mum but it was a terrible time between us. She was trying to look after me, but I didn't see it that way. She never sat me down and said: 'You could be involved in murder and drugs and all that goes with it. You could get killed.' She would just say: 'Your dad's a thug, he's this, he's that.' And I didn't want to hear any of it. I shut myself off from everything she was saying.

Auntie Rita and Salvatore were sentenced to six years each for drug trafficking. Nan's lawyers put in the appeal. Early in December 1987 they got out of jail. Auntie Rita was freed completely, while Salvatore was put on house arrest in Calabria. It was business as usual, life pretty much as normal for them. And several judicial contacts of Nan's had an extremely good Christmas.

When I heard of their release, I realised that although the family was not always immune, Nan looked after us all with the power of her imperfect morality.

And herself. In March 1988, just after my eighteenth birthday, Nan was released on bail. She moved back into her new three-bedroom Via Christina Belgioso apartment, which allowed more space for her activities. It looked like a high-street-store showroom, because everything was spanking new. Of course, everything was stolen.

She had chandeliers, marble floors and carpets so thick it was like marching through the jungle from one room to another. There were gleaming, wall-to-wall reproduction antiques, highly polished by some of the drug-dependent houseboys she had running around. She had a Florentine desk in her bedroom with drawers where she kept the few bits she considered precious, keepsakes rather than valuables. On top of the desk was her favourite item: a shiny black electronic bank-note counter. It was protected by her one indulgence – scores of perfume bottles, all shapes and sizes, from the traditional houses like Chanel, Dior, Fendi and Givenchy, gifts she'd collected over the years.

She'd gone high tech with the money machine because even her lifetime experience of counting cash with her thumb and forefinger, faster than the speediest bank teller, couldn't keep up with her cash turnover. This device counted the money and sorted it into denominations, great piles of notes kept in similar cellophane packs to those used for the tons of heroin.

Nan had her system, her priorities. Drugs were weighed in the kitchen by the baskets of aubergines and courgettes, cash in the more fragrant environment of her boudoir. For her, nothing would get in the way of her return to pre-jail life. Even the police in her home.

Ezio Dorigatti, the copper given the job of ensuring that Nan was behaving and living within her bail conditions, failed to report anything untoward. He wasn't a problem. Not for one minute. Why should he be? Nan looked after him. He was around the apartment most of the time and she fed him. In his early thirties, with a couple of kids, he complained about the money he was making and how difficult it was to make ends meet. She paid him handsomely. In return he ignored the drug dealing, and even concealed guns at his own home for the family and alerted her to any police action.

I was eighteen years and six weeks old when I telephoned Nan. I told her about Bruno. About Dad not speaking to me. About Mum going ballistic. How miserable I was.

Nan talked to Mum, who was finding it hard to accept that I was of age to go. But she'd known it was just a matter of time. It was her life repeating itself. In some ways it was a relief from the horrible tensions we'd had, which were so contrary to our true feelings for each other. It was a mother–daughter stalemate. Mum is made the way she is and wasn't going to change. I hated staying in England. She was always getting at me and we had no money. I'd had enough. I'd done a year of business studies but had no prospects. Everything I wanted in my life was in Italy.

When Nan said she would make a home for me in the apartment and look after me, Mum was in a corner. She didn't like it but there was nothing she could do. Nan sent me £500 for the air fare and 'a nice dress'. She made everything fine. She said to everybody: 'They are in love. Leave them alone.'

I got on the first flight, on my way to begin my proper Mafia apprenticeship.

CHAPTER TEN
MAFIA MAKEOVER

'I'm a good girl, I am.'

AUDREY HEPBURN AS ELIZA DOOLITTLE,
MY FAIR LADY, 1964

Bruno's grin when he met me outside baggage claim could have grated a carrot. I'd never seen anyone so glad to see me and I couldn't keep my hands off him. We were such new lovers we couldn't get enough of each other. He'd brought a bright red BMW to collect and impress me and with a big smile he drove it into the forecourt of a bed and breakfast place, where we spent the entire day in bed. I didn't notice anything about our surroundings. I didn't care about that. It had been a long time and we made love like there was no tomorrow.

That night he took me to Nan's. The next day Angela said she'd seen the car outside the B&B. She was laughing, in hysterics. She told me it was a knocking shop, notorious as the place the airport hookers took their clients. I couldn't believe it. I told Bruno it was a disgrace but he just grinned and shrugged. And what did it matter? There was a bigger problem facing us – Dad.

He was nearing the end of his time inside and was on day release at the bakery. He wanted to see us. Nan told me he still wasn't happy about Bruno and me but smiled: 'Don't worry about it. I told him, "They're in love. You can't do anything about it. They're together. What are you going to do?" I've sorted it out but you still need to see him. If you don't, there's nothing more I can do to help you.'

She'd done enough. Dad couldn't have been nicer to us. He hugged me. He embraced Bruno, but there was a warning in his eye as he told him, 'Be good to her.'

Nan was the star of this show. She'd made everything wonderful for me. I had Dad on my side and Bruno beside me. It was what I'd been waiting for. In England it had been difficult; I was missing my Nan and my family. I missed the culture, the lifestyle. And now I had it.

Nan was always giving me money for nice clothes, and I stood out. I was English and the Italian guys were interested in that. I attracted a lot of attention everywhere I went. But Bruno was my man – during the day at least. I would go to his house and spend a few hours with him, then I would have tea with his parents Giordano and Dina, who loved me. I got on brilliantly with them and his younger brother Dario and his sister Silvia. After tea I would go back home to my nan's.

At night Bruno would vanish to illegal gambling clubs and we girls would stay in and watch videos and get stoned. There was plenty of puff going around. We used to smoke the whole *panetto* [block of hashish], then we'd go in the kitchen and eat ice cream and, half an hour later, go and make pasta. There was me, Auntie Mima, Auntie Angela and her boyfriend Ricardo, who was allowed to sleep over but not in the same bed. We'd make a right mess in the kitchen and not clear up and Nan would go absolutely ape in the morning. She had a woman who used to come in and clean. We were just being lazy.

But Nan made us work too. She taught me, just as she had my mum, how to make hot tripe – which I hated – home-made meatballs with fresh tomato sauce, stuffed artichokes, risotto and fresh bread and cakes. She bought crates and crates of cactus figs and sat for hours picking the needles from them, sucking and shaking her fingers every time one cut her. This was *La Signora*. A contradiction.

She would get in the face of people who upset her and ask: 'What's wrong with you? Do you want to get killed?'

And for hours on end she would dutifully prepare fruit on the chance that her sons might want some when they came to dinner. And no matter how many turned up – twenty, twenty-five or thirty – it was Angela or me who had to clear up. The washing-up we had to do! We used to go mad because my uncles brought their girlfriends, and we'd be cleaning up after all of them. It was like a restaurant.

Lunches I didn't mind because Bruno was around. He'd become an operator for Nan, who used him the way she had Dad when he was younger. Bruno was put in charge of deals all over the city; he would 'mind' shipments and look after any dealer who didn't deliver or pay up. Once he and I were a couple, Nan trusted him more and more.

I was car mad but had never learned to drive. Bruno taught me in a new Lancia Delta Dad bought me. Bruno and my uncles sped around the city in Maseratis, Mercedes and Porsche sports cars as if they were in glossy motoring adverts. I just accepted that this was the life, which was going as fast as the cars. There was always something happening.

We used to go to clubs and be first in the queue. It was VIP treatment everywhere we went in Milan. At a mention of my surname, doors opened instantly. They'd know about me, and they'd know not to mess. Sometimes it was ridiculous, with Bruno or my uncles beating people up just because they dared to look at us across the roped arenas.

Even the police were wary. But they couldn't ignore us. Nan's early warning system was brilliant, and before raids anything incriminating would be circulated around the 'safe' neighbourhood apartments. Except for the money. Nan never let that go. The cash was hidden in the freezer inside plastic containers of frozen pasta sauces.

She was rarely caught off guard, but one morning I was still in my dressing gown, sitting in the kitchen sipping coffee, when she came bundling down the stairs from her bedroom.

'Take this! Hide it!' She handed me an envelope bulging with money.

'Where?'

'There.'

She was pointing between my legs.

I shoved it in my knickers and tied up my gown. I was stuffed with money.

She looked at me. 'Keep your mouth shut. And put your foot on that tile.'

She was pointing at the kitchen floor by my chair. I moved my left foot over the loose tile just as the cops waltzed in the front door. I was alert and just had to do it. I prayed they wouldn't force me to get up because the cash would've spilled out and the cops would have taken it; they wouldn't have reported it. But they didn't bother with me, a teenage girl.

And there was nothing to find elsewhere. They left after only fifteen minutes; it was as if they were going through the motions. After they'd gone, curiosity made me lift the tile and reach in. I pulled out a pistol. I've no idea what type it was but it was big, heavy and ominous.

It was the start of the most tumultuous times of my life. Shortly after the raid I found out about an arrangement to murder someone. Dad was finally out of prison and was back at the family table for the daily business meetings. I wasn't part of it but I was around, in and out of the kitchen as they talked, and that's how I heard.

The family had a friend, a guy who'd worked with the Camorra, the Mafia organisation which has infiltrated almost all of Naples and beyond, as powerful and effective as the Cosa Nostra and the 'Ndrangheta. An influential *Mafiosi* from the Camorra flew to Milan to see my dad and asked permission to murder this guy. He had to ask consent because it was my dad's turf. Dad couldn't have gone to Naples and just shot somebody. He'd have to ask and explain: 'This person has done something wrong to me. This is what he's done. He's taken it to the extreme. I have to show that he can't get away with it. If not, everyone else will do the same.'

I knew the man they wanted to kill. When Mum and I moved out of the Mussolini flats in 1979 my family – not the council – put this family in our place. They'd come from Calabria. So it was a bit more personal. It wasn't a guy I didn't know. What made it worse was that I knew he had a wife and kids. He'd wronged the Naples *Mafiosi* and Dad couldn't condone it. He couldn't save him. To be honest, Dad wasn't that bothered about it. If it had been a family member it wouldn't have happened. If it were someone he cared a lot about, it wouldn't have happened. But Dad and Nan gave the go-ahead. If they'd turned the request down it could have caused a war between them and us. That's how it was.

I don't know what was said, but I did know in advance it was going to happen. I was nineteen years old. I've had to carry that. I couldn't go to the police, and I couldn't stop my dad. What could I do?

A lot of the time I would bury my head anyway. I was quite happy living in my own little world. I was just a young girl. I didn't see into the future. I didn't see the seriousness. I know right from wrong, I can't deny that. It was my dad. It was my family. That's the difference. I can't explain it.

I was being pulled in, groomed in their ways. Unless you're put in a situation like that, you don't know how you'd react. I was a young girl. What was I supposed to do?

There was a lot of agonising about death. And the heroin trade. Uncle Filippo's girlfriend Alessandra and Auntie

Mariella had died, and Auntie Mima and Dad's youngest brother Alessandro were heavy users. A heroin addict with AIDS, called Rosolino, lived in Uncle Antonio's house and did housework for smack.

Nan would give them all heroin. She didn't want them getting it from anywhere else, stuff that might not be right. As a mother, she was stuck between wondering, 'Do I give it or do I let them go on the streets for it?' She was whispered about as *Mamma eroina*, Mummy Heroin. She purposely looked older than her age and others called her *Nonna eroina*, Grandma Heroin. She was killing them herself and she was probably killing other kids. It's a puzzle. She was so generous on one side yet this was her way of life, of living. She did not know what else to do.

When my dad got back from jail he said: 'This isn't life. We can't carry on, we can't carry on. People have died.' He also argued the commercial point. 'And there's not as much money in heroin.' He'd recognised a gap in the market and wanted to start dealing hashish. 'There's not much of it around – and nobody dies from it. This is the money now.'

There was soon a great deal of hash worldwide as Dad created a super-efficient smuggling empire. He was a very, very good businessman, the articulate one. He'd never had any schooling yet he'd made millions, and wanted more.

I knew what was going off. I can't hide that. Dad was flying around here, there and everywhere. And so was I.

On Dad's first hash operation in the summer of 1988 he sent me, Bruno, another girl Annie, and three strong-arm lads to Marbella with an expensive, big 7 Series BMW. The car was to be exchanged for merchandise. He forked out for all of us to stay in a smart hotel near the beach. I can't emphasise enough how to me it felt so normal; I didn't even stop and think about it.

Annie was there because she had a false document to say she was aristocracy. On your documents in Italy they put what your employment status is, then you can also have *bene stanti* – wealthy. Annie's ID had *bene stanti*. She was to take this ringer car over to Morocco when the time was right. But there were delays by the supplier.

One of my uncles had a bar in Marbella and we took over the town. I spent a full month there just waiting. I'd go to bed at 4 p.m., get up by midnight, have something to eat, go out until 8 a.m. clubbing and then go on the beach. That's how I lived. We slept on the beach and then went back late afternoon and we did that for a whole month.

We got to know the locals. The sister of one of Bruno's friends brought her lad along, who had recently arrived from Milan. I had very long hair and that day I'd had it all scraped back at the hairdressers', where they'd twiddled it around into a bun. It looked really sophisticated and I was wearing smart clothes as well. This lad, who was about our age, said, 'Who's she? Has she just come out of college?' He didn't quite call me a 'snotty cow' but he tried to take the piss, almost but not quite to the point where I'd be offended. I sat there amused by what he was doing. Then the sister must have said something to him about why I was there and who

I was with. He hadn't realised who I was. When he was told he absolutely shat himself: 'Oh my God, they're going to kill me.' He couldn't stop saying, 'I'm sorry, I'm so sorry.'

Finally, it was time for Annie to go across. She took the car as planned but they wouldn't let her into Morocco. She didn't look wealthy enough. She didn't have a delicate look about her. She just got turned back. It was all an expensive mess.

Naturally, Dad wasn't happy but he had already made a connection with two highly dangerous and well-connected dealers in Seville. They paid the way for the ringer cars, and the Morocco shipments began. He had teams working out of Marbella. Spain became home from home.

Dad never wanted anybody to know these guys in Seville. He was very protective over things like that. He watched out. They, the shadowy international competitors, wouldn't dare, but you never know ... Dad thought like the fictional 'Lupin' he was often nicknamed after by the Press, and was just as devious.

The Seville collaboration was golden, a bonanza, and the British market was one of the most profitable. Dad had a connection with a London gangland family we knew as 'Santos', who would fly over to Spain with payoff money, sometimes as much as £750,000 – and that was a down payment. There would be two further instalments of the same or more as required. And it was, as elsewhere, repeat business.

The Seville partners had to be paid too. I was recruited into the financial side of the operations. Bruno and I were to take the money and hand it over to the actual guys, the Mr Bigs.

Dad didn't tell me what to do. He just asked, 'Marisa, will you go and take that money to Seville? Are you okay with that?'

And I said yes. I wasn't nervous about the trip. I was too young to get scared at such things. Besides, I'm very adaptable; I've had to adapt wherever I've been. Some people find it hard but I had to deal with it. Once I'd made deliveries a couple of times, I was trusted enough but never completely. No one ever was. I had the ability to get from A to B, and I had my head screwed on enough to be responsible for the money. I always had an air of 'butter wouldn't melt' and Dad saw that in me, that I wouldn't raise suspicion. I was quite mature for my age. I always wore nice clothes. I didn't look posh, but I looked like someone who was well-off, middle class and spoke well. Dad would always going on about me being *rispettabile* [respectable]. I knew where I was going, and I knew what I was doing. I take after him in that way, thinking on my feet, getting myself out of anything that might be a problem and cause trouble.

It was like him taking Mum on the cigarette runs while she was pregnant, and while I was a baby. Women in the 'Ndrangheta are part of the game, always active, especially during vendettas and wars. When the men are under threat the women have to organise everything. Women are never war targets. During war times the men would often cross-dress to escape attack. Some of them tried to get away with long wigs but without shaving off their moustaches.

Dad used women's freedom to move around undetected for his drug trafficking and the payoffs and cash collections. People, including the police, didn't usually think of women, never mind young girls, as gangsters. They didn't enforce the same restrictions on us.

Tight dresses, short skirts and spilling cleavage were useful distractions when encountering border guards. Manipulation became a way of life; you go on a bit of a power trip. If I went by plane, I'd strap the money around me. I'd wear granny knickers, big Bridget Jones numbers, and lots of loose layers of clothes. The cash would be in plastic sleeves all over my body, from top to bottom. I was walking money, a cash Christmas tree.

For the amounts I used to take to Spain to pay for the hashish, security companies would use armoured vehicles. It was loads of *lire*, about £80,000 or £90,000 worth at a time if it was me on my own. If it were a couple of us, we would have that much each. If there was a particularly large amount of money, I went by car and it would all be put in the panelling. Bruno would do the driving because although I knew how to drive I hadn't got my licence. We didn't want something like that to cause a problem.

We could put up to £500,000 in a car and we'd motor gently across Italy, France, Spain – two borders, three countries.

Once we stopped in a hotel in France overnight, and I got the money out of the car and into my big cash bag. It was *lire*, packets of it worth up to about £250,000. The next morning before I took a shower I took it out of the bag and put it under the sheets for safety. I didn't want anyone walking in and nicking it.

I repacked and we were off, but in Seville I found it was about £13,000 short. I panicked: 'Oh my God!'

When I told Dad he was a bit suspicious. 'Are you sure, daughter of mine, that you haven't ... 'cos I'd rather you told me.'

It didn't matter who you were when it came to business: 'Dad! I swear ...'

I wondered if Bruno had taken it but he hadn't. We'd left it under the sheet. I must have missed it. I trusted Bruno. He wouldn't have taken it. He never had. He never did. There was no point. Why lose yourself over something like that, when you're making enough money anyway?

When I was back in Milan I phoned Mum and told her that I'd been moving some of Dad's money for him for tax reasons and a chunk had got lost. She was working as a chambermaid at the Imperial Hotel in Blackpool and with her innate Lancashire trust in the system she said, 'Hopefully the maid will find it. You might be lucky.'

More likely the maid would be. Of course it never did turn up.

I lost £13,000 but out of the millions I transported, that was the one thing that ever went wrong.

Often we drove straight down to Seville, a ten-, twelve-hour car journey on the dual carriageways. We'd go around the Granada region, through the mountains, and see trucks full of merchandise with the locals on their bikes hanging on the backs trying to get in to steal stuff. It was pitch black. We had far more money in our car than any of them could get in those trucks.

Bruno always said, 'They'd better not stop us.'

But we didn't have any weapons to defend ourselves. It was a risky business.

Bruno got badly hooked up on one Seville trip. We stopped in northern Spain, and he couldn't sleep because he'd taken so many drugs. He was curled up in a corner looking at me and telling me I was a witch. I thought: 'Oh my God, we've got all this money, about half a million pounds, and he thinks I'm a witch.'

Finally I lost it: 'What are you doing?' I shouted and shouted at him but he was out of it.

I've a rational brain. What if he'd killed me? They'd have found me dead in the room with all that money and then Dad would have killed Bruno. He never considered the possible consequences of being quite so doped up. But he slept it off.

Dad never seemed to sleep. He based himself in Spain and was always busy. The phone was either on his ear or in his hand every hour of the day. He'd doze off with it next to him. I didn't see much of him, maybe a day here or there, as he was moving around the whole time.

He was now the CEO of a growing empire with nearly 200 people working directly for him. He had contacts in Holland, France, Germany, Belgium, Switzerland, throughout the UK and in Colombia and America. The best routes were from Morocco to the UK and Colombia to Milan.

He was in constant touch with Nan in Milan. She was in charge of sales and distribution and was the tough negotiator. Even family members had to pay up front for their supplies. There was constant family rivalry. Dad's brother Antonio and his wife Livia De Martino were the most enterprising of my relatives, with a turnover of hundreds of millions of lire.

The family profits from narcotics trafficking – despite the deaths of Mariella, Alessandra and all the other people we knew, it still went on – were being invested in apartment blocks and shopping malls, being laundered every which way possible. Bank accounts were held worldwide.

I was at the centre of it now and events tumbled one after the other. It was like being on a rollercoaster – thrilling and scary all at the same time. But I learned not to break sweat, no matter what.

Even with the hard men of Seville, Dad followed the family policy. He cut out the middlemen and went straight to the source, dealing direct with the man known only as 'The Sultan', who controlled the growing fields of Morocco. He operated from the perfect climate of Cabo Negro on the Mediterranean coast in northern Morocco. And he was totally ruthless.

Dad went to Cabo Negro for a secret meeting and said: 'Deal with me and you will make more money. No payoffs, no middlemen. Only more for you.'

In return, he demanded the best hashish resin, thousands of kilos of it, five or six times purer than the normal consignments. When it was agreed and the profits soared, he got another nickname – The Kingpin.

And as his princess, I spent much time on the Costa de la Luz, the Coast of Light, across the Straits of Gibraltar from northern Morocco, playing evasive tactics with the high-spec surveillance copters and boats of the Guardia Civil and UK and Spanish customs authorities.

Yet the biggest concern was our competitors, particularly the French. They'd burst in and violently interrupt drug exchanges, killing who they had to and stealing the cargoes. Which is why people around me were very careful. They took precautions. They carried AK-47s. Some of them had Uzis as well.

CHAPTER ELEVEN
CAT AND MOUSE

'Those who'll play with cats must expect to be scratched.'

MIGUEL DE CERVANTES,

DON QUIXOTE, 1605

It was a deadly game that was played on the beaches and in the coves from Tarifa to Estepona, half an hour away from Puerto Banus. Along that south-east corner of Spain around the smuggling hat-trick of Morocco, Gibraltar and Algeciras, Dad's crews would wait for the drug drops. There would be shooters on guard but payoffs all but guaranteed nothing but the most unexpected interruptions. Yet it was nervy for everyone involved along the Cádiz corridor.

Incredible amounts of hash, tons and tons, and money, millions and millions of *lire*, were involved. In the moonlight the crews collected the hash like packs of flotsam from the beach, and put it onto the transport for Milan.

It was hard work psychologically and physically, with the waiting and waiting and then the loading. Often the hash would be hidden among catches of fish and these Spanish and Italian lads had to go in and get it out. They stank so badly they had to get rid of all their clothes afterwards. The dope packages reeked of fish. I'd smell it for days, like a bubblegum pop song that wouldn't go away.

Through a contact of his, Dad used holiday coaches. There would be real holidaymakers, Saga-type customers, on the buses. Their suitcases were stacked high on the false compartments hiding the drugs. It had to be spread around different modes of transport, because one coach could never carry it all; each delivery would be at least four tons, 4,000 kilos of hash. Some consignments would go by truck, smaller loads by vans and cars. The coaches proved the safest.

Dad was responsible for it all. If there were any mishaps and drugs were lost, he had to fork out. He was earning so much that a kilo here or a kilo there didn't bother him. The turnover was around one hundred billion *lire* a year. Every week Dad dispatched tons of Moroccan hash as well as cocaine to our beach collection points. There was a huge storage centre in Turin where the consignments would get divided. Whoever bought, even just a kilo, bought it with money up front. Family had first dibs.

Everybody talked in drug code. They had conversations that would mean little to snoopers, even experts from *Sisde*, the colourful Italian secret security service. Nan used to use the word 'clothes' for hash and cocaine: 'Go and get me those clothes from there. Just get me about three.' That would mean thirty kilos. 'Pasta' meant heroin. And Nan always spoke with her difficult dialect, which was a bonus.

Within two weeks the contraband would do a quick-change act and turn into cash. The operation generated so much money we had to have counting machines like Nan's, lots of them. It was the perfect business plan, a super-efficient corporate organisation. Dad was a multimillionaire and in the early 1990s he was at the top of the chain. But everyone had to play their part.

Hash was now the family speciality rather than heroin, but there were tragic echoes of that trafficking. Auntie Mima – daft, crazy Auntie Mima who'd had her way with Luis Miguel – died. She'd been abusing heroin so much her whole body gave in. She was only thirty years old.

Nine days later Uncle Alessandro, Dad's youngest brother, died from a collapsed lung brought on by heroin. He was twenty-nine. In the space of days my nan had lost two children through heroin. She dressed in mourning and carried on grieving for many, many months.

But so did the business. Including heroin. Dad had a Lebanese associate, who had connections in heroin trafficking in Syria. This associate was a major player, and one of his markets was Australia. He was astute and able to work with different Mafia clans, including the Camorra and the 'Ndrangheta. He would get heroin shipments of up to twenty-five tons to Australia through Gioia Tauro.

Collaborations like this were only part of the 'Ndrangheta network, which stretched way beyond Calabria with 'ndrina active in northern Italy and across the world in the UK, Germany, Belgium, Holland, France, Eastern Europe, America, Canada, Japan and Australia. Mafiosa from all over appear every year in San Luca for the annual 'Ndrangheta summit at the Sanctuary of Our Lady of Polsi. Nan gave a lot of money to the Sanctuary and each August we'd join the devotions and processions.

San Luca might be the spiritual home of the 'Ndrangheta but there was always secular business discussed in the shadows. It's the village leaders who recognise and approve foreign crime clans as officially belonging to the 'Ndrangheta. They're seriously powerful.

When Nan took the family to Milan it was these village aristocrats of Italy's ever-growing richest and deadliest organisation who gave their blessing and ongoing help. Family allegiance was everything. Which was why Dad, although furtively managing the hash trade, also got a heroin deal together with his Lebanese associate. They had history. Dad had to get the drugs to the Lebanese man, a huge guy who wore a kaftan and was always grinning. He looked like a genie in a cartoon movie.

When Dad told me the heroin was going to Rome and Bruno was going to drive it, I kicked off and said I didn't want him to do it. I worried that he would get caught. Dad said it had to be done. He'd made the deal. I was in love and devoted to Bruno so I said I would go with him. With two of us, a couple, it wouldn't look so suspicious. Dad agreed to that. Bruno said nothing.

We were in a smart, rented Audi, a family car, and we had my little black Yorkie, Jessie, and three kilos of heroin. The smack was purer than Jessie, whose mum was a white poodle.

After we had driven about half a mile towards the *autostrada* out of Milan, Bruno turned to me and said: 'We're not going to Rome. We're going to Madrid.'

I caught my breath: 'My God, we're going through customs.'

Dad had duped me into this trip by telling me it was to Rome rather than Madrid, but I never saw not going as an option. He knew a young couple had a better chance of getting through, and by then I had another advantage – a UK passport. I'd spent hours at the British Consulate in Milan to get it. It was a complete rigmarole, even though Mum was from Blackpool. I knew it would make life easier at borders and airports than my Italian passport.

It was late at night when Bruno and I got to the Italian border and the customs officer waved us over. He had a big, sniffing-in-the-air Alsatian with him. The doorway of the customs building was about a dozen yards from us when he shouted, 'Documents!'

I jumped out and handed them to him. For whatever reason, he didn't come right over to the car with the dog. My Jessie was squealing and jumping about. I could see him looking at the car, looking at us, and I asked: 'Do you know where we can change some money?'

'You can park over there, then come and change it here.'

Bruno parked and said: 'He's got a dog.'

I barked like one at him: 'I *know*!'

That dog was really agitated because it could whiff the heroin but the customs guard thought it was my Jessie he was interested in: 'He wants to play but he's working.'

The customs guy was easygoing, friendly, and told me again where to change the money. Bruno went in, sorted the money and we were off. It was a blur by then, just a relief to get away without the car being searched. Someone was definitely looking out for us that night.

Going to Rome from Milan is a three- to four-hour journey. You're in your own country and it's less likely you'll be bothered. Going across borders with dogs is altogether different. But things went smoothly at the French–Spanish border and we made it.

It was boiling hot when we got to the Lebanese man's office in Madrid, which was full of antique jewellery stashed in glass cabinets. He had lots of Egyptian bracelets and necklaces and said, 'Pick something you like.'

I chose a beautiful bracelet, which I've kept safe ever since. Maybe it's got a curse on it like something from *The Mummy's Tomb*. I've never been lucky with jewellery.

The cash turnover was running into millions and millions. We opened numbered current accounts in Switzerland, in Zurich and Geneva. To avoid footsteps in the money trail, couriers – often me – physically deposited the notes in safe-deposit boxes. I'd deposit around a million pounds sterling at a drop. The money would then be laundered through investments in Italian local government and real-estate companies – Dad had villas in Spain and Portugal – or used upfront to buy drugs and weapons.

Dad was on an Iberia flight from Madrid on his way to visit one of the Geneva accounts (and a lovely bank employee) when he met another gorgeous girl. She was three years older than me, tall and dark. She looked stunningly familiar, because she was a model and her face was all over glossy magazines at the time. Dad worked his magic. So successfully that she took him to meet her parents, a Dutch couple. Her father, Theodor Cranendonk, was a wheeler-dealer with businesses in Holland and Switzerland. He was known as a Mr Fixit. He and Dad had much to talk about. Dad went into bullshit overdrive and told some extravagant tales and he so intrigued Cranendonk that he was invited to their holiday home.

He said to me, 'Right, we're going to Klosters. You've got to pretend you've been to this smart school in England.'

He'd spun them a story about being a big businessman in Italy and that his daughter was a graduate of the UK public school system and could speak English really well.

I softened the situation. I was good cover. We stayed with them in their luxury apartment in Switzerland for a couple of nights and they were a lovely-looking family. The mother was particularly pleasant; the father reminded me of Robert Kilroy-Silk, the one-time MP and TV host. He was tall, in his early sixties and a very attractive man for his age. But not as nice as he looked.

He dealt in weapons, in armaments of all kinds, from pistols to tanks, rifles to rocket-armed helicopters. He was involved in scores of other international deals including the illegal dumping of radioactive waste. The Dutchman's endeavours had paid off. The turnover of his company based in Vaduz, the capital of Liechtenstein, was upwards of £3 billion a year.

The coincidence that this striking-looking model's father was one of the most important, and dangerous, arms dealers in the world was quite extraordinary. What made it more astonishing was that our relatives in Calabria had just recently pleaded with Dad to help get them more weapons because of a war that had broken out down there. Fate had presented another connection.

Yugoslavia was in a mess, with the separatists and nationalists as well as a string of other factions plotting and counter-plotting. Theodor Cranendonk was arming all sides. It was straightforward for him to divert weapons to Dad for the Calabrian war.

Initially, it was easily transported stuff – explosives, bazookas, Kalashnikovs. But there were ongoing pre-orders for even heavier action hardware, including lethally equipped helicopters. Cranendonk's going rate for an attack chopper was $1 million a pop.

One of the Dutchman's connections was a UK arms company, which was transporting weapons on to Kenya. That's what the false invoices said. They were enough to get the war weapons, including ground-to-air missiles and rifles and pistols of all types and brands, over borders and into Italy and nowhere else.

Hundred of millions of *lire* changed hands but there was also a 'goodwill deal' that Dad negotiated with the arms merchants. In return for free equipment he would grant them favours. Dad disproved to me in many ways the belief that you can't get blood from a stone.

Arms couriers mostly used cars with secret compartments, but some would simply store the weapons in bags in
the car or in the trunk. 'Official' shipments with clever paperwork would allow access to most of Europe. The UK–
Holland route was one of the most effective, with weapons
coming by sea.

Drugs were always good money. The profit margin on
arms was boosted by weapons shipments being mixed in with
stolen antiques, classic cars and even rare jukeboxes. One
shipment came with stolen motorcycles, Harley-Davidsons
from America.

I didn't know much about the Calabrian war at first,
until one day when Bruno and I were asked to drive a shipment down south to Uncle Domenico. It seems the fighting
was, as ever, all about power. Bruno told me about it on our
trip.

The De Stefano brothers, Paolo and Giorgio, had
appeared in the 1970s, when they got started in a small way.
No one had heard of them until they killed a man in Modena
for a fraud involving four oxen. The De Stefanos quickly
graduated. One of their most important henchmen was their
underboss Pasquale Condello, one of the killers in 1974 of
Antonio 'Uncle Tony' Macri. It was a controversial shooting.
Macri not only organised the Mafia in Calabria but worked
with legendary American Mafia figures, such as Frank
Costello, to help recruit Calabrians into the American and
Canadian Mafia. His death was trouble. More than 300
people died during a two-year battle, known as the first

'Ndrangheta war, and the De Stefanos emerged as one of the strongest factions in Reggio Calabria.

Nine years later, in 1983, the second 'Ndrangheta war began when Pasquale Condello's sister Giuseppina married Antonio Imerti, a local *'ndrina* leader. The Imerti–Condello union worried Godfather Paolo De Stefano, who thought his empire was under threat. He took preventive measures. He tried to have Antonio Imerti murdered.

The car bomb didn't finish Imerti. The revenge hit was more successful, and Paolo's life was over after he was criss-crossed with high-velocity bullets. Nan's Serraino family lined up with the Imerti–Condello clans. All the *'ndrine*, all the crime families in Reggio Calabria, were on one side or the other. Every corner, every shadow, could hide a hit man. Every time a driver started a car it could trigger a bomb. No matter how many precautions were taken and how many bodyguards hired, it didn't stop the killings.

My uncle Domenico linked up with Pasquale Condello, and the De Stefanos were backed by the powerful Tegano family. It was a long conflict of wills – and weapons. Our partner Condello was a ruthless adversary (four life sentences for murder, Mafia association, extortion, money laundering and drug trafficking) but was often on the run. The charges against him included the 1987 killing of Lodovico Ligato, a former head of the Italian state railways. So Uncle Domenico was often a hands-on commander. His opposite number was Domenico Libri. The families got into a round of tit-for-tat killings that took their toll on both sides from 1987 through to 1991.

They shot dead my godfather Demitri Serraino with a 7.63 calibre pistol as he sat in his favourite barber's chair waiting for a wet shave.

Then an explosive bullet from a high-precision rifle blew the top off the head of my dad's cousin, his *compari* Santo Nicola, as he left his house for the bakery. He had master-minded bomb attacks against our enemies but his own elab-orate precautions weren't enough to save him as he hurried from his front door to his armour-plated car.

Uncle Francesco was gunned down by automatic fire as he was serving wine in his café-bar. He wasn't even a soldier; he was murdered simply for being close to my family. For that they had 'spilled his guts', three shotgun blasts in his stomach and then two in the chest for gratuitous insurance, yet another victim of my family's bloody war.

Soon after, so was the man who ordered his assassination. The same .30-calibre rifle with a telescopic scope that had been used to murder Santo Nicola was fitted with a silencer and taken to kill lethal rival Pasquale Libri. Libri was in jail, issuing orders from behind bars, but being in protective custody didn't save him as he took his Sunday morning exer-cise in the prison yard on 18 September 1988. From a high building away from the prison walls, the marksman put a rifled, explosive bullet in his forehead.

This particular marksman rarely failed. The same day he shot dead on the street two other members of the Libri clan responsible for Santo Nicola's death and that of my cousin Francesco Alati.

With nearly 700 combatants and innocents already dead the violent vendetta was escalating every day. Which was why I was helping pack military weapons into the secret compartments of the family's customised Citroën.

My father had ordered me and Bruno, whom he trusted with his and my life, to transport this firepower from Milan to the battlefield in the South; we were riding shotgun – literally – to the little Calabria, to the home of the 'Ndrangheta, where I had spent many summers.

My Uncle Domenico was one of the key survivors in our *'ndrina*. He ran a pizzeria – it was quite funky for old-world Calabria, with a disco bar – but also our war. He was an expert with guns, he loved them. He appealed to my dad for help because the enemy were killing off our main men, so Dad went to Theodor Cranendonk and got the weapons and Bruno and I were ordered to take them down.

It was a ten-hour drive with me, a distraction in a tight dress, sitting almost on Bruno's knee because the weapons took up so much space in the car. At dawn we stopped at a Motta café, an Italian Costa Coffee. We were looking for a parking space when Bruno turned to me: 'Look at that!'

There were five *carabinieri* cars at this service stop. Now these are the big boys – when these cops are involved it's bad news; they are like the military police. What should we do? Drive on? No, that would attract attention. Instead we parked up right next to them and went in the cafe. The *carabinieri* were at the other end of the bar. Most ordinary people keep well away from them so by doing just that we weren't looking conspicuous.

We had coffee to wake us up a bit and a munch of brioche. By the time we were finishing the *carabinieri* were going out. They stood right by our Citroën, which was a few years old and looked like a car we youngsters could just about afford; nothing exceptional.

Except for the concealed bazookas, machine guns and the rest.

Four of them were standing by the car smoking and talking when we walked over. Nobody spoke. Nobody smiled. We got in, cool as you like, and took off like Bonnie and bloody Clyde.

We didn't stop again except for the bathroom, and by the evening we were at the pizzeria.

'Marisa, Marisa!'

Uncle Domenico hugged me and clapped Bruno on his shoulder. He was so happy to see us. He smelled of cigars and garlic, his teeth a sinister display as always.

'I'm proud of you for doing this, *you* should be proud. This is all in the family, for the family.'

The enemy had hit key targets, and it was bad. Their family and friends had been getting killed for months and months. If it was all in the family, with no outsiders, nothing could come back to haunt them: Uncle Domenico fervently believed blood does not betray.

Now he had his new guns. He wanted to celebrate after dinner. He said to Bruno: 'Do you want to go out and shoot in the mountains?'

Of course, Bruno, like a little kid, went: 'Yeah, yeah, yeah.'

They went off at midnight to shoot at signposts in the mountains. I suppose Bruno couldn't refuse, it was a testosterone thing, but I thought: 'Stupid bastard.' We had risked so much to get there with all that stuff. We'd made it safely and the idiot went out in the dead of night and could either get killed or caught. I was so upset, I burst into tears.

I wasn't upset carrying the hardware and guns all the way down there, but I was about him going out shooting. For target practice? For the sake of it! It's what they did to show fellowship, shoot bullets into the sky.

Men! Bruno? Stupid, stupid. But I loved him and that's why I was crying as he was shooting. Men, guns and love ... I didn't want to lose him. I might have been too young to understand the complexity of everything that was happening but I knew Bruno would be shot outright if the other side knew who he was. I was also aware that as my father's daughter I would be assassinated without a thought. That's why we only stayed for a couple of days as Uncle Domenico made his preparations and then he sent us off, safely back north to Milan, with kind words and lots and lots of cold pizza.

That's when the war intensified. The military weaponry we had brought down took things to a whole new level, where bullet-proof cars couldn't help, and the De Stefanos literally didn't know what had hit them when bazookas and anti-tank grenades came into play. Domenico Libri only just survived a bazooka attack organised by Uncle Domenico.

It wasn't all one way, though. Uncle Domenico drove around in a bullet-proof car with bodyguards, often disguised in dark glasses, a false beard and a wig. But patience paid off for his killers. They waited, played the clock, and then, in a break with his routine, Uncle Domenico showed himself. He strolled onto his bedroom balcony to smoke a cigar.

Suddenly, instantly, the assassins were ten metres away.

With 12-gauge shotguns the hooded shooters blasted him all over the front upper deck of his house. When I heard the news, I was in shock. That was horrid. He was a lovely, lovely man. He was one of my favourites; there are some you really like, some you don't, but he was wonderful, and within a few months of us taking the weapons he was assassinated.

The revenge attempt was swift. Giovanni Firca was a jeweller, known as The Goldsmith, and a money man for the other side. He was comfortable in his Nissan SUV, which was double, double armour-plated with extra layers of steel. Which is why the first bazooka round didn't smash it into pieces at Christmas in 1990. The second bazooka shot took out the front and the SUV burst into flames. Firca survived, God knows how, but many others didn't, hosed down with bullets, in the ambushes and battles that followed. It was a war zone, the *carabinieri* terrified of going in.

Every night in Milan I would overhear excited phone calls about the news from the South. The local police, understandably not too motivated, were always at the scenes *after* the events but found few clues. They did know one thing – the rounds used in some attacks were from a consignment of bazookas 'lost' in Yugoslavia.

Mum would get me going on the phone from England. I tried not to let her know about the deaths but she had her own information network within the family. I'd try and brush it off as all happening down south while I was in Milan. But every phone call was tense and we couldn't seem to talk properly. One of us always said the wrong thing that got the other going.

Once I dismissed her concerns by saying, 'It's just a vendetta, Mum.'

Just a vendetta! That's how everyday this life was becoming. The tragic and the violent was normal, something that happened every day of the family's lives.

Mum had witnessed it too. She knew in her heart. We'd have been better off not talking but neither of us wanted that. Mum always put my mind into overdrive. She never had to spell out her concerns. They were there from the moment she said my name.

My fears were always that I was going to be shot and die. I had so many people around me getting shot and killed. Everything was going so fast, the gun-running, the drug-running, the money-running. I was on a Mafia marathon.

I escaped back to Milan where Nan was sort of central control. She never lost track of anything. She stayed mostly in the North. She had to be careful, for even as a woman she'd be a big target, a killing prize for the other side. Instead, she sent the money – millions of dollars went into the feud – and arms. We bazookered our way to victory; it was the military hardware and cash that my father had sent to his troops that won this particular territorial war, that was over before my twenty-first birthday.

Meanwhile Dad was keeping Mr Fixit and, particularly, his daughter happy. We'd visit them and the bank accounts in Switzerland regularly.

On one visit I noticed that Cranendonk's daughter had a big rock, a Cartier Panther ring, on her finger, and I said, 'Your ring is nice.'

'Oh, your dad bought it for me.'

'Oh, oh, right.'

'I'm sure he'll buy you one.'

I was fine about it. It was his girlfriend, wasn't it? But she went on about how he would buy me one and that pissed me off. I thought, 'Shut up. Why are you trying to justify it?'

'Just be nice to her,' said Dad.

'Nice! She's horrible.'

I tolerated her but I was so rebellious that Dad would get mad. And Nan would tell me: 'If you were a bit nicer to your dad, you'd get loads of things from him.'

I was getting older and more sophisticated in what I wore – and what I liked. I had Cartier sunglasses. I bought myself a £1,200 padded Chanel bag. I had to have that. It was a tiny distraction for we had another battle on our hands – but closer to home, on the streets of Milan.

When I was a little kid playing around the Piazza Prealpi we used to mix with some kids along the street called the Pellegrinos. Auntie Angela and I and some of the others would play with them. The eldest lad really liked my Auntie Angela, and his brother fancied me. Everybody knew everyone else.

As they grew up they'd done well for themselves. They had a few quid, but money doesn't make respect. They got involved with a gangster called Victorio and made war with a gypsy group down from us on Via Aurelio Bianchi, which was rough. The gypsies had a lot of respect for my family. There were also Slav squads around, everyone trying to niggle into our family business. But Victorio was the man making all the moves.

In the middle of this, a gypsy lad known as Muto was killed. We never found out who was responsible or why. He was a bit loud and mad and he was tortured, run over by a car a few times and set alight. His brother wanted revenge but he got shot and all hell broke loose.

The Pellegrinos wouldn't mess with us and we wouldn't mess with them, but this Victorio got very ambitious. He just thought he could become 'The Guy', like the jumped-up idiots you see in movies; to imagine you can come from nowhere and get respect was fantasy. Yet we were in his way and he put a bounty on Dad's head.

It wasn't the first time, and Dad joked about his bargain death price of £100,000: 'Is that all I'm worth? I'd give him double that just to get lost.'

I didn't find it funny.

The war had returned to the streets of Milan.

It was only weeks before my twenty-first birthday. I was pregnant. I was getting married.

And rival gangsters wanted to kill us.

CHAPTER TWELVE
BETTER OR WORSE

'The Devil can cite Scripture for his purpose.'

WILLIAM SHAKESPEARE,
THE MERCHANT OF VENICE

Yes, it *was* like the wedding in *The Godfather* movie. It was tradition and tuxedoes. There was dancing and champagne toasts, the kissing of hands, the making of promises, the devotions to the family. Even a hit squad turned up. I could have been killed on my wedding day.

I was so in love with Bruno. We had our rows but basically he was good to me. He certainly wouldn't have dared to play around or he'd have had Dad to answer to. I was four months pregnant when we got married but I wasn't showing too much. I could have got away with a beautiful white dress in a church but I didn't want to take the mickey. I wore an expensive, specially made heavy silk and lace dress. It was lovely, the beige lace over a light brown dress for the ceremony at the registry office on 8 April 1991. Mum was there and Grandpa Rosario gave me away.

Dad couldn't do it: there was a price on his head and the police were still hunting him on a dusty arrest warrant. A cousin, Francesco, had died from a heroin overdose at my 21st birthday party in the February, and that had made Nan even more distraught. She was still in black and mourning Mima and Alessandro's deaths six months earlier. She was in no mood to celebrate. I could understand her not being there.

We took lots of photographs at Auntie Livia's house before driving to the ceremony in a Rolls-Royce, a gift to us for the day from good friends of the family. They also gave every woman an orchid.

It was a very straightforward ceremony but we had a big reception after in a fancy restaurant outside Milan, with around 200 guests. We had the Italian chef of the moment and, with Dad paying the bill, the best of everything to eat and drink. Dad had really wanted to come and I was devastated that he couldn't.

It was the correct decision. As Bruno and I were getting out of the bridal car at the restaurant, three killers on motorbikes waited in ambush. Two on one bike, one on the other, in a classic attack-squad set-up. The gunmen were stalking Dad and thought he was in the Roller with us. They were there to take a hit on him.

But the cops were there too. They saw each other. It was a stand-off.

The cops told us later: 'The gunmen realised we were there. As we saw them, they saw us.'

They thought they might have killed me if they had been given the chance. That would have hurt Dad and made him take risks.

It was tense, dangerous, and I started to become more aware of what was going on around me. I had to be careful in the car. There was a lot more security. I had bodyguards with Magnums.

And I had a home to make. Bruno and I had moved into an apartment Dad had bought for us down the road from Nan's. It was smart and modern, with marble floors and mirrored walls. We had bulging bank accounts and new cars every other week.

At first, although I'd been with Bruno for four years, Dad was grumpy about the pregnancy and acted like an Old World father: 'Why haven't you done it right? Why haven't you got married first?'

I said that I hadn't intended on getting pregnant, and I hadn't. He didn't speak to me for a month. Then he came round to it and did everything he could for us.

Dad was also in Milan, living in an apartment near La Scala opera house under an assumed name. I didn't know where he lived and neither did anyone else. With him was Valeria Vrba, who was now his number one woman. Like Cranendonk, Valeria's husband, who at this time went by the name Mario, was an arms dealer. He was a Sicilian living in a huge villa in Zurich and could get batches of Kalashnikovs – but not the military stuff, which was the speciality of Theodor Cranendonk. Dad was pleased to get what he could, where he could.

I never liked Mario but Dad went along with him. Mario drove a Ferrari and they talked cars. The Sicilian had something else of interest – Valeria. She was a Slovakian model and absolutely gorgeous, with blonde hair, which was curly at the bottom. They were all about the same age and liked each other. They used to come down to Milan with their two-year-old girl Etienne. Valeria was sweet and after a time I could see that the Sicilian made her life a misery. She and Dad became lovers and she left her husband.

She could only have done that for a man like Dad because Mario was one of those guys who would never let you go. He'd rather kill you. She saw a way out. Upped and left, took Etienne with her. Mario was devastated. He couldn't believe that his wife had left him for another man. This big, hard, macho man who deals in weapons came to Milan, got on his hands and knees and begged Dad to give him his wife back; begged him on his knees. Dad was shocked at the embarrassment of it. He said he loved Valeria and couldn't give her up: 'She doesn't love you, she doesn't want you. Let her go.' Grudgingly, he did.

Although I was heavily pregnant I was still doing currency runs. Who'd think a pregnant girl would have a million quid in her bag? Dad was also travelling and would occasionally see Cranendonk's daughter, who overlapped for a time with Valeria. On one trip they all met at Zurich airport.

Valeria on Cranendonk's daughter: 'She's an ugly cow!'

Cranendonk's daughter on Valeria: 'She's awful, plain.'

Dad stayed out of it – and away from his gangster rivals and the police. He kept on the move with Valeria, in Spain and Portugal where he felt safer, one hotel and then another. He was never in one place for long. When he did return to the La Scala apartment to deal with some business in the city, about fifty cops arrested him. They had tracked him. They knew he was up to no good but had no proof. He hadn't quite finished his manslaughter sentence; he'd just wandered off and by the time the red tape caught up it was a couple of years later. So they served their warrant and after a brief court appearance Dad was back in San Vittore.

His old wounds began playing up again. Nan sent a consultant into the prison to examine him. It was serious and Dad had to be hospitalised. Staff weren't told which hospital or on what day and at what time. He was taken to the renowned Fatebenefratelli Hospital in Milan. It was all high security.

Nan had the timetable to the second through the crooked consultant. We all knew from the outset. I knew the night before. I was anxious. Bruno was involved in it and got up about six in the morning. Eight men escorted Dad in hand-cuffs to the Fatebenefratelli on a Tuesday morning. It's an old hospital with tunnels underneath with long corridors. The armed escort used a side entrance to avoid the crowds. They didn't want contact of any sort until they got to the examination rooms.

A guard called Marco threatened Dad: 'If anything happens, you'll be the first one to go down. I'll shoot you.'

But Dad's escape team, who weren't any older than me, were more co-ordinated than the police and prison service. They were dressed in surgeons' gowns especially lifted from the hospital laundry. They knew Dad would be brought up the stairs, not by the elevator. That he wouldn't go past the third-floor reception area but through a corridor behind the desk. They were all armed with side guns, pistols. And they had a couple of stun guns, which were the latest gangland gadget.

In the consultant's corridor – it was need to know and they had no idea the doctor had been got at – they pounced on the escort team. They sprayed their faces with tear gas and knocked them silly with the stun guns.

Marco the guard got flustered. Dad ordered him: 'Take the cuffs off now.'

He didn't get on with it: 'Are you going to have a go now? You going to kill me?'

Marco peed himself while one of dad's 'surgeons' grabbed the keys and unlocked the cuffs.

They rushed down the back stairs of the hospital and through the underground corridors to a waiting bus, a huge holiday coach from a drug-trafficking contractor. Dad climbed into the false compartment, where food and water were waiting. Twenty-one hours later when he got out he was in the south of Spain.

The escape was a sensation. The surgeons' gowns, the surgical precision. Afterwards when the Milanese talked about the Fatebenefratelli they'd joke: 'Ah, there the Godfather makes the cuts.'

The Italian newspapers went on about the 'electric shock guns' for they were a novelty. Even the police didn't have them, and here was some divvy dropping one in the hospital corridor as they escaped. They reported it was the first stun gun in Italy. A picture of it was on the front pages.

That day in Milan I shut the blinds, got in my car and drove to Rimini. I knew the police would be knocking on the door, they'd be hassling me. I'd have said nothing. What *could* I tell them? I knew it was going to happen but not the details. Well, not all the details.

Just before the escape I had been in touch with Bruno using the world's new device, my mobile phone. It was a millionaire's toy costing upwards of £2,000 a time. Mine was like a car phone, but it came in a little handbag you could carry around. Dad and Bruno had international ones that the FBI used.

As I drove to the seaside, knots in my stomach and my heart beating faster and faster, the search helicopters buzzed around above me. The manhunt was on. I never got a call saying: 'It's all right, it's done.' There was radio silence; you just didn't risk it, even with the brand new mobile temptation.

It's a three-hour journey down to Rimini and Bruno met up with me there that night. It was about midnight and we were still out. Everybody who was involved in getting Dad out came to Rimini and we drank champagne and had this massive restaurant feast. We were absolutely over the moon and happy that they'd done the job and Dad was out.

About 1 a.m. we got a call from Dad: 'I'm fine, I'm here.'

There was a big cheer in the restaurant. Not only did they free him, but 'Lupin' was safely gone, another miracle escape performed.

The newspapers were full of it and yet again it was San Vittore prison that, indirectly, he'd escaped from. It was still embarrassing. They absolutely hated him for it. It was like a massive slap in the face for the prison and the police. It was a long, hot summer for them in 1991.

I kept away from Dad in case I was followed. When it was vital I was able to speak to him. He was in the Seville area at first and then moved to the Costa de la Luz, to Jerez de la Frontera, close to the border with Portugal.

I was still doing currency drops right up until it was time to make a baby run. Military service was compulsory for boys in Italy and although I was 99 per cent certain I was going to have a baby girl, I decided to give birth in England just in case. Even at 99–1 odds against having a boy who'd be eligible for conscription, I'd learned not to risk my family on anything other than 100 per cent guarantees. And guarantees with insurance at that.

I was feeling the August heat in Milan and near the end of the month, when I was eight months pregnant, Bruno and I got in a sensible Volvo station wagon and headed for Mum's. We arrived in London late at night and were sitting at traffic lights when a car pulled up with four black guys in it wearing gangster hats.

'What's going on?' Bruno asked me, worrying that it was a set-up. He had to be ready to look after Emilio's daughter and first grandchild.

I said, 'It's all right. That's how they are here.'

We headed quickly out of the city.

I went for check-ups at the Blackpool Victoria Hospital and went through all the preparations. One night a friend of my pal Dawn's, who'd met Bruno on his last trip, took him out for a drink. They went to a pub in Blackpool where a bloke had a bit of a go at Dawn's friend. Bruno eyed the situation up. He didn't speak any English, but he got the idea.

When the bloke who'd taken the mickey went for a pee, Bruno went into the toilets after him. He slapped him up against the wall and stuck a flick knife under his neck. Pressing in with the knife, he snarled in Italian: 'Don't take the mickey. I know what you were doing.'

Then Dawn's friend walked in – this was his local pub – and exclaimed, 'Oh, no, Bruno. You don't do that here.'

But as far as Bruno was concerned, this guy needed sorting out. That's what he was like. You did not disrespect. His friend was being disrespected. But in return, out of respect for his host, he let the bloke go; white-faced, the troublemaker hurried off leaving most of his pint behind.

My daughter Lara was born after eleven hours of labour on 11 September 1991, her father Bruno's birthday, at Blackpool Victoria Hospital. Everyone followed the script. For me it was a long but simple birth. Bruno was the proud dad, preening away. Mum was the stereotypical first-time grandma, all love and fuss. Dad was also true to form, being on the run and in hiding. But he was desperate to see his granddaughter. It was a risk but Big Brother surveillance hadn't yet blanketed the world so we decided to take her over to him.

Lara was a month old when we flew to Malaga. Bruno carried out lots of checks first and we took a long route around to Dad, who was at that time in Porto Santa Maria between Cádiz and Jerez. When we got there I found out that Valeria was pregnant with a new sister for me!

Lara was a handful, and Bruno was not much help. Dad sent him off on business and I was left to cope. I couldn't sleep, I hadn't slept, I was turning into a basket case. Dad could see I was upset. He had on one of his smart suits and he lifted Lara, wrapped her in a blanket and put her on his shoulder. He rocked her a little and she quietened down. Then he got on the phone, explaining to me: 'I'm getting a nanny. I want you to get some rest. I'm going to get someone in who'll stay up with Lara.'

It was two weeks of restful bliss for me with the nanny and Valeria, who was so good, to help. Dad introduced me to Chinese food. I'd never eaten proper Chinese before because Mum couldn't even afford a takeaway, but I loved it. I loved my dad, and the fact that he seemed able to fix everything for me, to make me safe and happy.

With Valeria pregnant, Dad was trying to find a family fortress. He planned to set up in Mozambique because they had no extradition treaty with much of Europe. He could retain his authority and still run his empire from there. It's a sort of outlaw country and, with many Italian residents, a home from Rome. Business was booming. Couriers were bringing in all the major drugs from Germany, France and Spain, and zillions of ecstasy tabs from Holland. They were importers and exporters of the best heroin, cocaine and marijuana available. Their customers were global. In partnership with a London gang – who often dropped off million-pound instalment payments – Dad was supplying a huge percentage of the hash sold in the UK.

He had lots of organisation to do before he could make the move to Mozambique. For the time being he based himself at his villa in Albufeira, in Portugal. Between October 1991 and July 1992, he was jet-setting from the Algarve on a false passport. All over Spain and Portugal, Italy, Slovakia and, of course, making money visits to Switzerland. Which is where we went for the New Year. We spent Lara's first Christmas with Bruno's parents in Milan and then drove off to bring in the New Year of 1991 thousands of metres up in the Alps.

Valeria was used to a luxury lifestyle from the gun-running profits. She skied, knew her way around resorts and yachts, the jet-set and the wet-set; she had a well-developed appetite for the high life. She'd persuaded Dad that the only place to be on New Year's Eve was Badrutt's Palace Hotel in St Moritz.

Bruno wasn't so sophisticated. We accidentally headed off to Saint Maurice in France, got lost for three hours, and only our 4x4 Lancia Integrale got us through the thick snow. We finally arrived late at night in the grand reception area of Badrutt's Palace. It was gorgeous, like a palace on the side of a mountain. Valeria had booked all the rooms using false documents. I'd now got Marisa Merico on my UK passport. Dad was Giovanni Roberti. There were no Di Giovines at this celebration.

On New Year's Eve, Lara was being looked after by a nanny in the room – the hotel had an 'approved' list – and Bruno and I were wandering around all dressed to the nines. We'd had dinner and there was a big function going on for the residents of the hotel. Pregnant Valeria had gone for a rest.

One of the guests partying there was Adnan Khashoggi, who for the previous decade had been known as the richest man in the world. He was a happy zillionaire that New Year: a US federal jury had only just acquitted him and Imelda Marcos of racketeering and fraud. Dad was impressed by his business – and his lifestyle. Khashoggi operated everywhere and had companies in Switzerland and Liechtenstein to handle his commissions.

With him at Badrutt's Palace was his one-time brother-in-law, Harrods owner Mohammed Al-Fayed. And there was Dad chatting away to them. They had no idea who Dad was for he used his name of the evening, Giovanni Roberti.

'Ah, Italian! I bought the Ritz in Paris from your country-men,' Al-Fayed said.

Khashoggi joined in and they all began talking. Before they moved on, I heard Dad saying: 'Let's keep in touch.'

It was a great holiday, but as 1992 wore on I was too afraid to go and see Dad. The fuss over his escape from prison had not dissipated, the drugs were still pouring in from Morocco, and he had at least four police and security agencies after him. There were a score of fugitive warrants for his arrest.

I did go and see my baby sister Giselle after she was born in Zurich in June 1992. She was a beautiful baby. Valeria couldn't use the Di Giovine name on her birth certificate so she used her own name. It was about four weeks before Valeria took Giselle to Dad in Portugal but I went back to Milan. I was still afraid for him. A lot of my family – my cousins, my uncles – were going up and down on business trips. The cops followed them and that's how they caught up with Dad in Albufeira on 31 July 1992, as part of Operation Kingpin.

The Portuguese, Spanish and Italian police all arrived – more than 100 of them on the doorstep – and arrested everyone at the villa, including Grandpa Rosario, Uncle Guglielmo and Valeria. Luckily, Valeria's mum Aurelia was there and she could look after my little sister Giselle.

We were in Sardinia on a three-week holiday. Bruno's sister Silvia, Auntie Angela and her boyfriend, and a group of others were there with us. When we got the call about Dad's arrest they all looked at me.

I left Bruno and Lara there. Lara wasn't even a year old but I knew Silvia was great with her. I flew to Milan to get money to bankroll whatever I had to, and caught another flight down to Lisbon. I'd never been to Portugal in my life. I stepped out to the taxi rank at Lisbon's Portela Airport and looked for a youngish, hungry guy at the wheel.

'I need to go to the Algarve, Albufeira.'

The driver was delighted. He wanted a few hundred quid and I offered him more. I needed his help. I had the name of the villa but nothing else, not even the street name. It was big news that this great Italian Mafia guy had been arrested five days earlier. I was paying in bundles of *lire*. The taxi driver must have known.

Dad was still being interrogated in the cells in Albufeira three days after his arrest but they let me speak to him. Among all his stuff they found Mohammed Al-Fayed's business card with his private number on it. They had to check Al-Fayed out, but when they saw he was legit they left him alone.

Valeria had been released. She decided to get out of Portugal as fast as she could so she left Giselle and her mother and flew to Vienna. She just went!

Dad was in the same clothes he had been arrested in. He was wearing a necklace I'd bought him for his fortieth birthday a couple of years before, a twenty-one-carat gold chain with tiny balls of gold on it, and that was sweet, important to me.

He seemed flustered: 'Help the baby, help Aurelia, but just be careful ...'

He told me where the villa was. Aurelia was in her late sixties and frightened to death. She had the baby to look after and her money was running out. No wonder she was delighted to see me.

But I thought, 'You know what? This is too much. I'm not staying here. What if they come and arrest all of us?'

Valeria's mum didn't speak Italian or English. She had a Slovakian passport but Giselle was on her mother's passport. I thought: 'My God, how am I going to get this baby out of the country?'

We had a solicitor in Malaga who was very well in with Dad and at midnight I paid the taxi driver to take us to Spain. As we drove, I planned it. Giselle would have to be Lara at the border so she could get through on my passport. We rolled up with this old Mercedes belching diesel and handed over the two passports. Giselle was asleep.

The customs guy asked, 'Baby, Lara?'

'Yes, yes.'

We were in Malaga at 6 a.m. Within a couple of hours the lawyer was on the case, Giselle and her Nan were asleep in a hotel and I was on the phone making more arrangements. Valeria moved fast when I spoke to her. She was in Bratislava but through our contacts we managed to get Giselle her own passport. Within a week I had her mum and Giselle on a flight to Slovakia.

Dad expected to be on a flight to freedom. He'd been taken to a high-security prison between Lisbon and Oporto, and Bruno had been to check out the area. He'd done a helicopter reconnaissance. While I was looking after Giselle and her grandma, Bruno was planning to spring Dad from the jail. It was simple – they were going to go in shooting and whisk Dad out by a rope ladder dangling from a helicopter. He and Dad did a $1 million deal with Theodor Cranendonk for an armed chopper and a platoon of mercenaries to provide the distracting firepower. It was all set up but something in the prison kicked off and the guards found out about it and the helicopter escape didn't happen. Dad remained in jail.

I was twenty-two years old, with a baby daughter. I also had a baby sister I felt responsible for. And Dad. And Bruno. And Mum in England.

The political and police pressure was on us all.

There was an international business to run.

And I had to face up to men who'd think nothing of shooting me dead.

CHAPTER THIRTEEN
LA SIGNORA MARISA

Tutto è permesso in guerra ed in amore.
[All is fair in war and love.]

ITALIAN SAYING

I needn't have worried. Like any good CEO, Dad had a system in place. He could run the business from wherever he was, whether in a horrendous Portuguese jail or in an outlaw haven like Mozambique. Deals were still going down and there was merchandise and money to deal with.

Yet my head was spinning. My priority was Lara. I went to see my mum, to my little getaway. Blackpool had never seemed so welcoming.

Bruno went to southern Spain to pick up the pieces and keep the operations safe. If rivals thought we were vulnerable they'd have tried a very unfriendly take-over. They were always waiting in the shadows.

The year before I'd put 10,000 US dollars into the Midland Bank Trust Corporation on the Isle of Man to cover a rainy day in Blackpool. Then there was all the money in Switzerland. Among the accounts at Coutts in Geneva, Dad had set up what he called a 'trust fund' for his children. It was a busy account. I'd put a little more than £1.6 million through it in a calypso of currencies. Dad had dipped in and now there was just short of $400,000 left. I had to act fast or risk it being lifted by the cops after Dad's arrest. I opened up an account with Mum at the National Westminster Bank in Cleveleys near her home. A local businessman, a friend from my teenage years, gave me a reference as a favour, without knowing what was going on. The transfer of $385,211.54 went all the way around the world, including Nassau in the Bahamas, before it got to Cleveleys on the Lancashire coast. I wasn't trying to be clever or devious about any of this; it's how bank transfers worked in 1992. It took two weeks to get there and by then I'd left England.

Mum and I had spent 2 September at the beach and had an early night with Lara, then Bruno's mum called around 2 a.m. to say that he'd been arrested. A lad in Spain had contacted her to let her know that Bruno had been picked up by a police squad in Malaga on 7 September.

Dad, and now Bruno! It was his twenty-fifth birthday and Lara's first birthday on 11 September. Bruno was going to come to England and we'd been planning to celebrate with a party at Mum's. Instead, I was with Lara on a flight from Manchester to Madrid, where they'd sent her dad from Malaga. I had a long black-and-white flowery dress, and Lara on my hip. It was boiling hot and the prison was disgusting, one of the worst prisons I've ever been in. At the visitor contact point I couldn't see where he was. We had to talk through cut-outs. We couldn't touch each other, could only hear each other's voices. Lara was sitting there with me and I burst out crying.

Bruno muttered, 'Don't get upset. Please.'

I couldn't afford to stay upset for long. I was on permanent prison visits for the next eight months to see both Bruno and Dad. I kept everything together, from Milan to Blackpool, because Nan had her own problems, ducking and diving with her deals, and she never left home any more.

I didn't want the 'trust fund' money to sit around in the NatWest. Mum was a signatory to my account so I got her to pick up the money. She went on her second-hand 1986 Honda Spree moped, which had one of those Miss Marple baskets on the front while the rear end belched smoke. It always needed a service. She went and got the cash and stuck it in a zip-up bag in her moped basket and brought it home again.

We'd found a massive metal box with a lock in the loft and when the cash was put in there I paid £1,000 to someone I could trust to look after it in their home. I invested £10,000 of the money into a garage business with my girlfriend Naima's husband James. I wanted to help them but also to legitimise myself and show an income source, as a silent partner in a business. I put another £10,000 in the Bradford & Bingley building society.

In November 1992 I started looking for a house to buy, and by the following month I was the owner of 7 Sheringham Way, Poulton-le-Fylde, Lancashire, which cost me £89,950. Cash. Now I had somewhere for Lara and me if we needed to escape. It's an address I will never forget, but I didn't live there straight away as I was still based in Milan.

Every weekend I would fly to Madrid on Friday night and on Saturday I'd visit Bruno. In the evening I would fly to

Lisbon and see Dad on the Sunday then I'd fly back to Milan. Once a month Bruno and I would be allowed a conjugal visit. He'd bring the sheets from his cell and they'd lock us in a room with a toilet area for two hours and let us get on with it. I felt sorry for Bruno and I still cared for him as the father of my child, so I would close my eyes and imagine we were on a beach somewhere rather than in a prison cell. The theory of conjugal visits was that they gave the men an incentive to behave inside. Most of them didn't. Being Madrid, there were a lot of Colombians and they all but controlled the prison.

Bruno wanted money and weed. On a visit they'd strip-search me; they'd look around in my bra and I had to take my knickers off but they didn't search me internally so I used to put the dope for Bruno in a condom and insert it in a tampon. He'd put it in his pants, between his balls, or in a cut-out in his trainers with the inner sole covering it. With the money he'd pay the guards and get them to buy cigarettes for him. Anything else he wanted, the Colombians could get.

Bruno's parents looked after Lara during my weekends away. They were kind and comfortably off people and were in shock because of what had happened to their son. They didn't know what had gone on, although they might have had suspicions because we obviously had a lot of money. For young people to have so much didn't seem possible. Unless there was something illegal going on. Which, of course, was the answer.

And I was now in charge of it. On my visits Dad would give me instructions. My voice was my dad's voice. I was running the organisation through him. I had the help of a lad called Mauritso, a friend of Bruno's. Dad trusted him and had a lot of respect for him. Mauritso was like a *capo* running a crew of other trusted guys.

Dad would tell me: 'Get them sorted. Get that done.'

I could easily have made up my own instructions and they would have followed them to the letter.

With Dad inside, my uncles were doing their own thing. And so was Nan. I was walking around giving orders. My Uncle Antonio had prospered but never had as much respect in the family as his brother. Now, with Dad out of the way, he wanted to muscle in. I had to watch my back with my own uncle.

There's a recording in which he threatens me: 'Tell her to do what I say or I'll pull her fucking head off. I'll pull her by her own ... I'll kick her up the arse ...'

My response to this was simple: 'Who does he think he is? I'm not doing anything he says. I'm speaking for Dad – you'll all do what I say.'

These grown men, who in their ruthless world would think nothing of pulling out a gun and shooting you, had to agree: 'Yes, Marisa.' They had respect. Whatever I said, went. They would have killed for me. That's the sort of people that I had around me. They cushioned and protected me.

Nan was very much a wheeler-dealer and tried to take advantage of the situation: if she could make another buck out of Dad she would have. In a complete turnaround, I was now lending money to her because too many of her deals were going wrong and she had overstretched herself.

In their minds they thought I was just a young girl but I wasn't having any of it and the people around me weren't either. They were loyal to my dad. They had a lot of respect for my nan but ultimately it was what I said that went. Not what my nan said. And certainly not what my uncle said. Nan started calling me *pazzesco criminale* [crazy criminal].

My most important jobs were retaining my dad's authority and making the right moves with our money, especially the investments in Switzerland. With that, I had the help of a very smooth operator called Fabio. He was a refined guy who didn't raise suspicion. He wasn't family, he was business, but he was trusted with collecting money. He escorted me to the bank accounts.

He was especially good at Coutts, the Queen's bankers, on Quai de l'Ile in Geneva. I placed an astonishing amount of cash there in hard currency – US dollars, sterling, *lire* – in specific currency accounts Dad had set up with the help of the two Seville middlemen. This was one way in which he laundered money from his drug-trafficking profits. There were also some safe-deposit boxes for emergencies.

Every time I went through the Swiss border I was taking money in or out of the country. I went through Lugano by car as the Italian–Swiss border was minimal risk and flew on to Geneva. When I first went after Dad's arrest it was to make a huge withdrawal: a quarter of a million pounds sterling alone was going to Valeria. I took Lara with me. The cash was in US dollars and the bundles were bigger than I expected. Remembering the photos of me as a baby lying on packs of Marlboro, I lifted the cloth on the bottom of Lara's carrycot and beneath it was perfect to fit these seven sealed Coutts packs of cash. In this way I carried Lara and a hell of a lot of money out of the bank.

I used to try and make a point of staying over, because it was gorgeous in Geneva, but sometimes I had to get in and out in a day.

On my next visit to Dad, he said: 'You'd best go to the deposit boxes in Zurich. Valeria's mum has a couple. See what's happening with them.'

Valeria couldn't risk leaving Slovakia in case she was arrested so I met up with Aurelia, her mother, again. When we got there, the bank manager said the boxes had been cleared out by the police. I was as wild as shit. What if that had happened to the 'trust fund'? We stayed at the Mövenpick Hotel and we were having a coffee in the hotel café when I realised we were being spied on. I was in a compromising position and the police could have arrested me then and there but for some reason they didn't make a move. I got a flight direct to Milan.

That experience changed me. I woke up to more things, became a bit more devious, more streetwise. I had to learn to judge people, to see through them to their real motives and intentions. I started to listen to my instincts if I didn't get a good vibe from someone. I learned to judge people straight away – but I didn't always control my power.

Lara and I were living in my apartment in Milan and we used to drive to Bruno's mum's every day for lunch or dinner. One night I got back about 11 p.m. and was about to park when a young girl stole my spot.

I jumped out the car. 'What are you doing? I've got the baby in the car. I was going to park there.'

She snarled and gave me the finger.

I was furious and I called a lad who worked for me: 'Get round here and puncture all her tyres. Do them all. Don't ruin the car but ruin her tyres.'

He came round an hour or two later and did it. It was no problem. I didn't go too far and get her car burned out, which I could easily have done. At least I stopped there. I know I shouldn't have done anything at all but when someone does something like that or talks to you like dirt, you can suffer a bout of road rage.

In March 1993 I was on one of my weekly visits to Dad. On the way back I checked my bag in at Lisbon for the Milan flight and while I was in the departure lounge I called Bruno's mum to check up on Lara.

'Marisa, don't come back,' she said. 'They've arrested your nan, your auntie, your other auntie ... they're arresting everyone in the family.'

I looked up at the constantly flicking departure board and a London flight was listed. I feigned a medical emergency and got my bag off the Milan plane, then I flew back to England, to Mum.

But Lara was in Italy.

I couldn't go back to Milan but neither could I stay in England without my daughter. There was no way. It would be better getting arrested than being kept from my daughter, me in one country and her in another. I had to risk it. They was no way I was going to be without her. She was just a baby.

I booked a flight to Nice. I told Bruno's parents to bring Lara to a spot that's just over the French–Italian border and said I'd meet them there. I bought a dark wig in Blackpool, telling the saleswoman at the seafront dressing-up shop that I was following my husband as I thought he was having an affair. They'd be on the lookout for blonde-haired Marisa Di Giovine. In Italy when you get married, you keep your maiden name. I was Di Giovine on my Italian ID papers, Marisa Merico on my English passport.

I wore the wig at Manchester Airport but at passport control the official said, 'You look so different in your picture,' so I gave up on that idea. I was drawing attention to myself. I left the wig in the toilet and put my hair in a French plait. From Nice I caught a train across the border into Italy. We met up, I had Lara in my arms and within half an hour I was back on the train.

It was nervy at Italian–French customs on the way back. Lara was on my British passport. The border guard took forever looking at us and at the passport because it was Marisa *Merico* and Lara *Merico*. He thought I was a single parent; in Italy a mother wouldn't have her child's surname. If the passport had said Marisa Di Giovine I'd never have got Lara out. He would have asked: 'Does her father know she's leaving?'

It was the longest few minutes of my life. I prayed Lara wouldn't say anything in Italian. She did say something but it was just toddler talk.

The guard said: 'English, yes? Daughter?'

'Oh yes, daughter.'

'OK. OK.' Much, much more than OK.

I'd felt physically sick standing there but I acted cool as a cucumber. I've got a split personality. I can be a bit devious in that way; I've had to be to survive.

In the carriage, two lads were smoking away and I resented that around Lara but I didn't want to move. I just wanted to stay in that spot and get to Nice.

When we arrived it was too late for a flight to England that night. Money was no object and I got our cab to stop at the first great-looking hotel on the Promenade des Anglais, the Hôtel Negresco. I sat on the bed half the night staring at Lara as she slept and thinking, 'I've got my little girl. Thank God!'

As I dreamily reran events in my head, everyone in the family who'd ever looked the wrong way was getting arrested in the police's Operation Belgio, named for my nan's street, Via Christina Belgioso. The manhunter was Maurizio Romanelli, a sort of Eliot Ness-style 'Untouchable' prosecutor, who dealt exclusively with the Mafia. He'd worked hard: wiretaps, seized consignments and documents combined with testimonies from people who turned state's evidence.

The star turn was Santa Margherita Di Giovine, my Auntie Rita, the woman who'd opened up her home to me and my romance with Bruno. She'd recently nicked 1,000 tabs of ecstasy from me to sell on to pay off her brother, my Uncle Antonio, who was cutting up rough with her over a drug debt. She'd lost him a lot of money and she was, quite rightly, scared of him. She was also on speed and schizophrenic. She was wheeling and dealing. He was ruthless.

Rita was fragile and not just from her amphetamine addiction. From childhood she'd been treated badly by my nan. She didn't have her own character. She bowed down. She was very jealous. Mum never got on with her. Out of all Nan's children, Rita was the one who always had to interfere, push herself to the forefront and get all the attention. She got all she could ever want after she was arrested in Verona for possession of the ecstasy tabs. She was caught, and couldn't face my uncle, couldn't face prison. Her son Massimo was an expert heroin merchant, and also a teenage addict. She would only have done a couple of years in prison, maybe more as a member of an organised crime family, but instead she started blabbing. She'd been inside before, and she couldn't face it.

It was the jackpot for Prosecutor Romanelli because Auntie Rita had seen it all. She was a living diary of the years going right back to when Nan moved the family from Calabria. She may have been strung out on drugs but Auntie Rita's memory of events, of dates and details, was sensational. She went back a long way: as a twelve-year-old she was packing heroin for transport, and her later jobs included bribing cops for protection and information. She'd kept the heroin accounts for Dad, she'd slaved for her brothers and Nan – the grass did not grow any greener than Auntie Rita.

Others grassed as well. Fabio, the charming gentleman, was picked up and became another *pentiti,* a state witness. He was pressured and he collaborated and as a right-hand man he knew a lot. Several in-laws gave in to pressure and felt obliged to talk.

One of them was an auntie's husband. He was a nasty piece of work anyway. She decided to go along with him, because they had three children together. I know that if she had had a choice she wouldn't have gone along with him. Everybody was arrested and she had nothing left. She would have been left to bring up her kids on her own. I understood in a way why she did that. He was her husband and she loved him, although it wasn't right what he did.

And Valeria's former husband Mario the Sicilian took his revenge on her and Dad. As soon as he was picked up he turned informer, which was no surprise to me. I was always suspicious of him. But he also somersaulted the cops and escaped to Brazil before some arms-smuggling warrants caught up with him.

But the biggest and by far the most important talker was Auntie Rita. All over Italy, Spain, Holland, Portugal, the UK and America, leads and contacts she grassed about were being followed up. Arrests were constant. All in all more than 100 *Mafiosi* officers and soldiers were picked up.

When I phoned Bruno's sister Silvia in Milan, she was able to tell me that there were forty-one family names, but not exactly who was on the wanted list. I might be next. What would happen to Lara?

By the morning after I rescued Lara from Italy, I knew I wasn't on the warrant for the mass arrests there, but what about in Spain or Portugal? I didn't know. I couldn't go to Dad, couldn't go to Bruno. Or my nan. I didn't move. I didn't know what was going on.

I sat in the hotel in Nice for a day, thinking.

The web was so complex and tangled.

I slipped through it.

I called on the one person who always gave me unconditional help and love – my mum.

She said she would open the windows and freshen up the rooms at 7 Sheringham Way, Poulton-le-Fylde, Lancashire.

CHAPTER FOURTEEN
RAINY DAYS IN BLACKPOOL

Tinemu d'occhiu u scurpiuni e u sirpenti,
ma nunni vardamu du millipedi.
[We keep an eye on the scorpion and the serpent,
but we do not watch the millipede.]

SICILIAN SAYING

Although she was just used as a drugs dogsbody – albeit a well-paid one, banking the equivalent of £40,000 twice a week – Auntie Rita's confessions brought the roof in. She knew the secrets, the devils in the detail. She told how all the kids had learned the code of silence, *omertà*, at Nan's knee. The lesson was not to tell the truth but to say nothing. Certain attitudes infiltrate throughout the Mafia lifestyle: honour must always be respected, family revenged.

I remember Rita talking about a Calabrian boy who died during one of our summer holidays in the South. She'd grown up with the boy and 'cried for a week' at the news of his death. But our male cousins did not. All they wanted to determine was who was responsible because they, in turn, were going to die. Three days later the killers 'weren't around any more'.

This story is like a perfect précis of a life that I was part of but I'd been able to rise above by timing and circumstances. Rita's brothers were their own deity, gods, while she and her sisters were regarded as no more than sex machines who did the domestic chores. She pointed out that if my dad went to Nan and said 'I need a million *lire*' he would get it, but Nan wouldn't buy her a new pair of shoes no matter how much she begged. That was the mentality, she said, passed down from generation to generation.

As Auntie Rita talked into spinning tape recorders, and some of the family plotted her assassination, I was setting up home in the north-west of England.

Sitting with Lara in Nice that night, watching her sleep so peacefully, I'd realised fully my responsibility for this separate human being. Without me, what would she do? When it all kicked off it was clear the safest move for her and me was going back to Blackpool. I had to balance my loyalties to Dad and Bruno, and naturally, as any mother would understand, it was no contest.

It wasn't returning to an old life; it was starting a brand new one as a single mum. In Italy, the slow arm of the law was working against the family and the evidence was considerable. The prosecution was painstakingly building their case on the pages and pages of confessions, a Mafia manifesto.

In the early 1990s there was a credit crunch in England. Everybody was skint. I had the cushion of hidden money, but I was careful. I was more Yorkshire than Lancashire about the cash, for I'd seen how fast it can vanish. I was really calm and settled because I didn't have to travel. My life was all before me. I had my house. Lara was becoming more a person than a baby, a real personality. It was mother and daughter time.

Bruno and my dad telephoned collect every week and that was my greatest expense – £500 phone bills. Otherwise

I didn't live an extravagant life. I just got my shopping. Mum and I would potter around with Lara. She was still working at the Imperial Hotel.

James, the friend in whose garage I'd invested money, helped me get our car from Italy, where I still had lots of stuff. A couple of motors had been impounded but there was still a sports Clio in Milan. I got Bruno's mum to fill up the Clio and his cousin drove it to the French side of Geneva, where he lived. I paid James to fly to Geneva, pick up the car and drive it across to the UK. I gave him all sorts of documents but no one asked for them; he drove it straight through.

So we had transport. I went about my own business every day. I paid my taxes. I paid my poll tax, my property tax. I didn't know when or if I'd see Dad or Bruno again. I couldn't dwell on any of that, because it was creating a future for Lara that mattered.

In March 1994 I got a job as a barmaid at The Golden Ball pub in Poulton-le-Fylde. It was a couple of nights a week, seven hours at £3.05 an hour, which they paid in cash. After handling millions in cash I wanted to get a sense of money in the real world. And I enjoyed it. The landlord was a nice bloke and the customers were mostly fun. It got me out of the house and I had cash to buy treats for Lara.

On 1 June 1994, a nice Wednesday morning, there was a knock on my front door at 7 a.m. It was the start of what they grandly called Operation Matterhorn. Customs and Excise were there to arrest me: 'We have a search warrant, you are under caution now ...'

But I had Lara! I told them I'd take her to my mum's. They said that wouldn't work because they'd already arrested Mum. She was at Blackpool Central Police Station.

I asked them to take me and Lara to my friend Naima's house but when we got there other Customs and Excise officers were searching it. I muttered 'I'm so sorry' to her and James. I was mortified that I had brought that trouble to their doorstep. They were straight people.

With Lara listening, the officer barked at me: 'Right, we're going to take you.'

I put Lara down. She held out her arms, sobbing 'Mummy!' It broke my heart, looking at her so upset. I just walked out of the room with the sound of her screaming for me ringing in my ears. That upset me far more than the arrest.

After the problem of what to do with Lara was sorted, I didn't say another word. In the newspapers it was reported I'd said 'I'm saying nowt' – but I didn't. I knew better than that. I wasn't going to say anything at all until I knew exactly what it was all about. They put me in an interview room at Blackpool Central and the duty solicitor was called in. With my good luck it was a brilliant solicitor called Trevor Colebourne, a man who understood the seriousness of it all better than me. I was distraught. I was being asked about 'offences regarding drug trafficking, benefiting from the proceeds of drug trafficking and money laundering'. When Trevor arrived for the formal interview to begin at 1.40 p.m. I still hadn't been charged. I'd decided I was going to try to blag my way out of it but he instantly talked me out of that, saying I shouldn't comment because whatever I did say might be twisted and used against me.

Along the corridor they'd started questioning Mum forty minutes earlier. She loves a good chat and her conversation with them ran for about 100 foolscap pages of transcript.

What I said didn't fill two pages: a couple of 'yes' answers to formal questions, my date and place of birth. It took exactly two minutes. The customs guy Roger Wilson was quite abrupt.

He had trouble opening one of the audio tapes for the recorder and I giggled.

Trevor tried to cushion this by saying, 'I think Marisa finds it quite amusing.'

I wasn't being spiteful or taking the mickey. It just came out because it was genuinely funny. By the time Roger Wilson got the tape open he was bright red. He got going and was about to ask me about my house when Trevor said it was going to be 'no comment' from then on and he was furious about that.

Mum was along the way entertaining his colleagues. They asked her about her marriage and the family in Italy and about the money transfers. Then, and later, I believe they got quite exasperated with her. When Roger Wilson interviewed her it was to do with a 'missing' quarter of a million dollars.

Wilson: 'There's still about 250,000 unaccounted for.'

Mum: 'Yeah, I mean … she went on holiday.'

Wilson: 'But hang on, Patricia.'

Mum: 'She wasn't working.'

Wilson: 'Quarter of a million we're talking here, it's not chicken feed.'

In turn, Mum got annoyed when they quizzed her about picking up the cash from the NatWest in Cleveleys.

Roger Wilson was the laborious quiz-master again: 'I mean, let's face it, not everyone walks through the streets of Poulton-le-Fylde or Cleveleys or anywhere for that matter with the equivalent of about £65,000 on them at a time in cash, that being roughly the equivalent of $100,000 US. It just doesn't make sense.'

Mum: 'I was on the moped anyway.'

Wilson: 'Was it an armoured plating [sic] moped?'

Mum: 'No, just on the moped and that was it.'

Wilson: 'Anyway, let's go on.'

Mum: 'I couldn't get a taxi 'cos I couldn't afford a bloody taxi!'

They charged me, fingerprinted me and shipped me off to Risley Remand Centre in Warrington, Cheshire. At 'grisly Risley' they gave me my jailhouse number, RG0991, and I became a statistic in the prison system. But a high-profile statistic, a big number.

When I got to the reception at Risley there were a group of others being processed. One girl said she'd been accused of harming her child and another girl started beating her up. Guards came and broke them up and I was thinking: 'Holy shit!' I'd only just got there. They took them off to the hospital. They said they thought I was vulnerable, did I want to go to hospital too? I reckoned it was better to be in the mainstream than with them.

The inmates all watch you walking onto the wing. It was spooky and intimidating. The first night I was bunked up with a black Brummie girl who was really nice and reassuring: 'It's all right. You'll be fine.' To my great relief, I heard that Mum had been released after the day of questioning and was back at home looking after Lara.

When they unlocked the cell, we had twenty minutes to get dressed and fold everything at the top of the bed as if we were in boot camp. I queued for breakfast with a plastic plate, knife and fork, which weren't very clean, and this bloody big girl and her friend were eyeing me up. I'd never been in prison. It was a huge shock and I kept thinking, 'Oh my God, I'm on my own here.'

I stayed out of everybody's way. On remand you don't have to work; you can just stay locked in your cell, and that's what I did most of the time. I got paranoid when I had to go out for a shower because I always had the big girl eyeing me up.

One girl tried to ridicule me: 'What are you in for? Didn't you pay your poll tax?'

But I got friendly with a prostitute who knew how to handle things. Everybody knew her. My solicitor gave me fags on visits and I gave them to her.

She said, 'See them walls? That is the worst it will get for you. The walls.'

I already knew what she meant.

I spent two weeks in Risley before I appeared in court in Blackpool. Trevor Colebourne was there and afterwards he told me: 'Marisa, I've got some good news and some bad news.'

I can't recall the good news. The bad news was that I had been designated a Category A prisoner – that's top of the line, number one villain, baddest of the bad. And I was going to Durham jail on remand to await my trial for laundering drug trafficking profits.

It was all guns then.

Everywhere I went the police were armed.

They took me to Durham as a Cat A, handcuffed to an officer and sitting on a metal seat in a blacked-out, armoured minibus with a sick bucket in front of me. It was a sweat box. You'd get done for taking a dog in it. There were police on motorbikes and a helicopter monitoring us sweeping across the Pennines through Scotch Corner to Durham. The escorts switched with the police jurisdictions. No vehicles were allowed on the motorway anywhere around the van.

We pulled right into the women's wing, 'H' block, through about five doors. They were all locked manually apart from the big steel outside one. It was a prison within a prison, home to Britain's most high-risk women, and they called it Hell Block.

Not all women were Cat A prisoners but it was *the* high-security area with lifers, child killers, paedophiles, any long-term prisoner doing ten years or more. I knew life was going to be like that Pink Floyd song 'Living in a Fish Bowl'.

Every fifteen minutes they'd shout my name and wanted to see me on the landing so they could check me off in the book. I was on suicide watch too. They had male guards, which I thought was weird – men with women!

The head bloke got a couple of girls to show me around: 'They're Cat A, like yourself.' They were two IRA bombers and they took me everywhere, like head prefects.

I know it sounds daft but it took ten days in that single first-floor cell for me to understand where I was and how serious it was. And then I thought, 'Oh my God. I'm never going to get out.' I broke down and sobbed my heart out. I'd stayed so strong in Risley, but in Durham I was on the floor, on my knees, in terrible floods of tears. The reality of everything hit me, especially of not being with Lara. I missed her so badly. I could cope with being contained but not being without my daughter. That's what made me break down – but what kept me going as well.

After an hour or so I got up and swore to myself that for the sake of Lara I'd simply get on with it. I was wallowing in my own self-pity. The trial was still to come and I was pleading not guilty. Maybe I'd be back home soon.

But meanwhile I was stuck in the claustrophobic atmosphere of Durham. Yet the roof was all glass and a lot of daylight came through. Obviously the higher you were, the more daylight there was, so most people yearned for the penthouse suite. I was lucky enough to get a top-floor cell, with a view of Durham Cathedral, one of the most wonderful buildings in the world.

Fun and sun *Baywatch*-style for me and Bruno in Spain in 1987 and 1989. We weren't in Marbella just for a suntan, but we did find time for each other on the beach.

On the run in the sun: Dad and Valeria escaping from the pressure at his villa in Spain, August 1991.

Dad dressed to be ill? That's him 'recovering' in Parma Hospital, 1987.

Mrs Marisa Merico – our wedding day. Little did Bruno and I know that there were rival Mafia gunmen prepared to spray bullets, not confetti, at our marriage celebrations.

Here I am, pregnant with Lara, on a night out with Dad and Valeria in Spain after his spectacular escape in Milan.

Back in the UK in August 1991 with Bruno – and with Lara very much on the way. I wanted my child to be born in England.

The following year I'm back in Italy – with baby Lara in a Milan park.

Daddy's girl: Bruno playing with Lara at home in Milan, 1992.

Three generations of the family – Mum, me and Lara – in Milan, 1992.

The Merico Bakery in Milan, the business Bruno turned his back on to work with my dad. Here I am with Lara and her dad's mother and sister.

Not too far from his family bakery, Bruno was doing well in prison – celebrating success with some baked goods of his own with the football team. After his team won the prison league trophy he was interviewed by a local television crew in a city where football is a religion.

In Durham Prison with my friend Lisa Corah (on my right) and two of the other girls, Maria (with the beehive) and Julie.

My faithful friend Naima was a regular visitor at Durham Prison and her presence always brightened me up.

Me, Mum and Lara on a prison visit at Durham with Linda Calvey, who was known as the 'Black Widow' and was one of the longest-serving prisoners in the system. With her is her friend Danny.

15 October 1999, the day Frank was released from Doncaster Prison. On the way to Blackpool we stopped at his brother's home in Leeds where they'd laid on a welcome home party.

Lara, Frank and my half sister Giselle, Dad's daughter with Valeria, who came to stay with us for a visit from Slovakia in late 2009.

My mum took this moody photograph of me and Frank in January 2010, when she wasn't well and I had no idea what the new decade would hold for our family. Change, for sure – I hope only for the better.

We only got an hour a day outside. That's if we were lucky. If it was raining, the officers refused to go out. We used to go mad. By law you're supposed to have an hour a day of fresh air. We'd say: 'We'll go out in all weathers – get some huts out there for the officers to shelter in.' But we didn't make the rules. That hour to us was everything. We would have gone out in rain or shine or snow. At Christmas 1994, it was gorgeous. The flakes were enormous. It was dead still, and in that yard it felt like heaven. We were walking all over and making prints in the soft snow. It was cold, but it was nice and still. I remember it clearly in my mind. It was eerie, and it was also emotional because we all missed our families, who were outside.

Sometimes I used to look up and use my hands to shield my eyes so I couldn't see the wall. I'd pretend I was looking at the open sky. I used to dream of going out at night and standing there in the dark to feel the night air.

I was given £1 a day and I saved it all up to buy phone cards, which were £3 a time. Every night without fail I phoned Mum and had a word with Lara, but as a Cat A prisoner I could only use one particular phone with a recording device on it and I had to tell the screws when I was ringing so they could listen in. That was tough. And Mum and Lara were only allowed to visit twice a month, which wasn't nearly enough.

I wrote to Bruno and poured my heart out. I'd had enough. Basically I said, 'I'm fed up with you. I don't want to be with you any more.' Being arrested, being in jail, made me free to tell him what I genuinely felt. He was part of my life but I couldn't see us being together forever. The depth of feeling, that special closeness, had gone. Outside, I would never have left him. I would always have been there to support him. I would have been obligated to. I always had as a wife. I couldn't have abandoned him while he was in jail and I was outside, but now I was in the same boat.

Our love relationship was over. It hadn't been working before he was arrested, for all the old reasons. He took a lot of coke. I didn't see him for long periods of time. He'd be out until four in the morning. He just wasn't a family man. He was devastated when I told him how I felt but we agreed to keep writing to each other. His mum came over to Durham and went to see Lara so there was still a lot of connection there. But it made me feel even more lonely, having cut off that link to my husband, one of the men who was supposed to look after me.

I got letters from Dad as well, but because I was Category A they were thoroughly scrutinised and I had to be very careful about what was said.

I got my head down and tried to get on with the practicalities of life in jail. We had bank accounts people outside could put money in so we could buy our own food. The auxiliary officers would go to Sainsbury's for us. I'd make a shopping list and off they'd go once a week. There was a fridge and you stuck your name on your stuff. It was better to make your own because the servery food came from the men's side of the prison and you never knew what they'd done to it before it arrived.

I began spending about three hours a day in the gym, where I met Linda Calvey, who was one of the longest-serving prisoners in the system. She was known as the 'The Black Widow' because every man she got involved with was soon either dead or in prison. I thought she was nice enough. She had a cloth with white lilies she used at the dinner table and she made a point of telling me that Reggie Kray had sent it to her.

I also got to know a girl called Beba who was in for terrorist offences and was still running a business on the outside. Then I met a Maori girl, a hit woman from New Zealand, who got nabbed on one of her first jobs. Before that, she told me she'd worked as a nanny and spent the winter of 1991–92 as a resident on-call nanny at Badrutt's Palace Hotel in St Moritz; she was there when I was and could have ended up looking after Lara, which was a big freak-out for me.

And there was Zoora, an Indian girl who was in for poisoning her husband: she got twenty years. She made me my first curry. In Italy we didn't have curry so my first-ever curry was made by Zoora who'd poisoned her husband. It was so spicy I'd never have known if she'd mixed arsenic instead of chilli powder into the chicken madras. She claimed she hadn't killed her husband but they all say that in there. The only one I did believe didn't do it was Sue, Susan May. She was convicted of battering her eighty-nine-year-old aunt to death. She became like my mum in there. Susan would help anyone.

Durham was the last stop before Rampton, where all the true misfits were sent. But we had some all the same. One

231

who was only about my age looked like a Honey Monster because she used to scrub her face with a Brillo pad until it was raw. Lots of them would find stuff with which to self-harm; a snapped-off plastic spoon would do it.

There were occasional big family visits. We'd go in the gym area, set up tables and the families would arrive. Normally, there were only eight tables, so there was only room for eight visitors at a time. If the visiting room was fully booked you'd had it. No visit, no lifeline to the outside.

The family get-togethers were great. If I'd spoken to my mum about someone in there she'd get to meet them. We'd be at our own tables, with our families, while the kids played in the middle with some toys. Day to day I would focus on my next visit. It was the only way. We all looked forward to it.

However, we hated the fact that the nonces were there, prisoners who were paedophiles or child killers. They stayed on one side with their visitors. Rose West was one of them and I was surprised to see that her kids came to visit her. They'd testified against her, she got life for abusing them, and yet they were still visiting her. It was spooky seeing her son because he has Fred West's face. Unless he's changed it or gone abroad, he's out there somewhere with that notorious face.

Security was high on family visiting days and once it was almost called off. One girl who'd killed three kids she was babysitting for – she set fire to an airing cupboard and when the house went up she left the children in there – set a fire in one of the education rooms. We were all excited and getting ready an hour before the doors were to be opened for our families and she torched a room in an attempt to set the prison alight. We wanted to kill her. If the fire had taken they would have cancelled visiting time completely, even though there were families coming from all over the country. They had to lock that girl in because we wanted to lynch her. We would have done. I would have battered her to the point of death, I was so mad. Then I'd have been in there for murder. Manslaughter. She was an evil, nasty piece of work. I don't think she had anybody coming. She never had visits. She only had a volunteer prison visitor.

We calmed down afterwards when the visit went ahead. That girl was stripped of everything. She wouldn't look at anybody. I left it at that. She was doing her time, that's her punishment. The prison didn't need me to punish anybody else.

I sometimes think back and wonder how I coped with that time. But every case is different. It's a mistake to judge too quickly on the inside, as it is on the outside. And those in for life had, literally, to live there. I couldn't bear to stay in the same room as child killers. I might have liked to have taken a crafts class but that's where they went. It was open to anybody, but I knew the nonces were going and I wouldn't go because I couldn't sit there with them.

You were in a prison within a prison already. You were very confined. How could they segregate you further on top of that? The women who were there were going to be there for a long time and they tended to think, 'Right, you know what? I'll just pretend she's not here. There's no Rose West, no monsters.'

The most notorious nonce of all, Myra Hindley, was sharing 'H' wing with me. I knew all about her. Mum was always reading about murderers and serial killers and, living so close to Manchester, the Moors murders had been part of our lives. There was always a story on the TV or the papers about the search for a body on the Moors. Or some hope that Myra or Ian Brady, who killed the kids with her, would pinpoint the burial spot of the little boy whose body they never found.

Oh, I knew who she was. But not the moment I first saw her. I'd grown up with the image in my mind of the blonde hair and that horrible, dead look on her face. When I first saw her, she walked past my landing using a stick. Her skin was yellow from the Golden Virginia roll-ups she smoked all the time. She ignored everyone around her. She walked purposefully on.

People wonder how nonces can walk around without getting kicked in by someone every five minutes. There were several like Myra in Durham, those who had killed children or burned people alive. It was hard to live with them every day. If you stopped and thought about it really deeply, your head would be mashed: you couldn't cope with it.

People have said to me: 'I'd have done her in.' It's human nature. They killed innocents who couldn't defend themselves, so maybe you should hurt them in return. But you can't. In such a close environment you'd be the one who would suffer. You would be the one who wouldn't have any visits. You'd be the one who couldn't phone home every night. That was my priority. Whatever I felt, whatever I wanted to do, what stopped me was the fact that I knew I needed to hear my daughter's voice every night.

For Myra Hindley, the other inmates didn't exist. There was an arrogance to her, as if she was regimented into pretending we weren't there. I watched her, I couldn't help myself. It was only a glance. She looked at me from my feet up for a split second, and then looked away. It made me shudder, hoping she wasn't looking at me in a weird way. I was still a young girl myself, only twenty-four when I arrived in Durham.

I learned from the lifers that the best way was to keep your head down and do your time in the easiest way possible: without getting your morals and your rights and wrongs in the way. For there's no black and white, only grey. As I found out when I heard the stories of some other inmates.

There was Maria, who was inside with her friend Tina, a couple of harmless-looking young girls. Except they were killers. In Wales, they'd gone to this old lady's house, a woman they knew, tried to get money from her and kicked her to death. It was a noncey thing to do, you don't kill an old person.

'We were on Valium,' they told me. 'We were on this, that and the other to the point where we were totally out of control, out of our heads and had no idea what we were doing.'

It wasn't an excuse but they were actually nice girls to get on with. They were a similar age to me and I had a laugh with them. I couldn't think about what they had done. They were sorry for what had happened. Had they been knowingly nasty and evil it would have been different. If you believe in God, then you believe that everybody should have a second chance. It's an instinctive thing; you either like someone or you don't. Tina and Maria were just normal girls. They had committed a horrific crime. But I would put my hand in a fire and swear they wouldn't do anything like that again.

What astonished me in Durham was how such normal-looking women could be inside for such incredible crimes. Sheila was inside because she set fire to her ex-boyfriend and the girl he was going to marry. She got her new boyfriend and his mate to kidnap the couple. They tortured them, tied them up, splashed petrol on them, torched them and shoved them off a cliff in their car. They didn't stay around to see the couple jump out, roll around the grass and live, although they were horrendously burned.

We were all in Durham when the papers reported that the couple who survived the attack had got married. We knew Sheila wouldn't be happy about it and worried that she might cause problems but she was just very moody that day.

She had a tendency to take out her frustrations on Susan May, the one accused of killing her aunt, taunting her that she was guilty, which always wound her up. Sue had a friend-ship with a guy in the men's side of Durham who used to send her sneaky sandwiches with a little message inside. It cheered her up but it was against the rules, and one day Sheila shopped her. She was like that. She was mean.

Once, just before lock-up, she pointed at me aggressively and said, 'I'll see you tomorrow.'

I looked at her, took my Cartier glasses off and said: 'No. You'll see me now!'

She tried to look away and I snarled, 'You'll see me now.'

The officers were chanting, 'Come on, lock up, lock up.'

I said to her: 'That's convenient, isn't it? Come on, what is it you want?'

She made up some pathetic response and backed off. She was quite a strong girl. She was petite, but she worked out a lot. By then, I did and I was bigger so I would have hurt her as much as she would have hurt me. She'd have come down with me.

I also had trouble with a child killer who looked like a creature from *Planet of the Apes*. She was blonde, blue-eyed and freaky-looking. She'd smothered one of her partner's children but the guy gave up his other kids to be with her and still visited her. Once she's out, if he's still with her he won't be allowed to see his children. I couldn't believe that man would still have anything to do with her after she killed one of his children!

She was in the servery one lunchtime. I couldn't stand her and I didn't like the fact that she was serving my dinner. We could bring in our own porcelain plates from the outside, although we weren't allowed proper forks and knives. This woman gave me some lip and put rubbish on my plate and

I thought: 'Stupid cow.' The lunchtime duty officer was looking out the window and didn't see the aggro building. I held my heavy plate like a frisbee and threw it at her face. It hit her hard, then shattered on the floor. I was glad. I didn't care. I knew they couldn't ship me out to another prison because nowhere else would have me.

The funny thing was, I didn't get into trouble for that. They never put me in solitary. They never locked me in my cell. I always seemed to get away with things. I never kicked off. I was a pretty good prisoner really. They knew that if I ever kicked off, there was a reason, and I wouldn't be doing it every five minutes.

Everyone reacts differently in an institution. And weird stuff happens. We all had a period at the same time. How strange is that? And imagine the tension?

Ena, a Dutch drug smuggler, asked for vibrators for all and the officer laughed: 'We'd can't do that – it'd be like a swarm of bees in here. *Buzz, buzz, buzz.*'

One night somebody got hold of a load of ecstasy tablets and they had a party in the television room. I didn't take any because I didn't want to be crawling up the walls. I had some hash and got stoned at the back of the room instead, watching all these girls get off their faces. They stripped to bras and knickers and danced to rave music. The walls were dripping with sweat; it was like a steam room. Not once did the screws come. They turned a blind eye.

Finally, finally, after more than sixteen months on remand in Durham, they finalised the case against me and gave me a trial date – 20 November 1995. The Italian courts were still hosting members of the family. I probably could have made it into the *Guinness Book of World Records* as the person with the most relatives in prison.

They moved the case against Mum and me to Newcastle Crown Court for security in case I might try to intimidate witnesses. Or stage a dramatic escape. But I only wanted to get home to Lara. And make sure Mum didn't go to jail. Her health was really suffering with everything. The cops didn't understand any of that.

There was a police escort for the trip to and from court. Station wagons at the front and rear of the van. The police in the cars had automatic weapons trained on the van. Sirens were blaring and helicopters were trailing us, like noisy vultures in the sky. At court, officers were armed with wicked Heckler & Koch MP5 single-shot, three-burst carbines. They said it was unprecedented. Apparently, they thought the Mafia might swoop in with armed helicopters and free me.

The week I went to court in Newcastle, Rose West went on trial at Winchester Crown Court. The Geordies got their geography wrong and, thinking I was her, chucked eggs at the armoured van that took me to court. I could understand that.

On the Wednesday, 22 November, Rose West got ten life terms for murdering ten women and girls, including her sixteen-year-old daughter, her eight-year-old stepdaughter and her husband's pregnant lover. She and her husband Fred West were charged with killing a dozen people altogether but he escaped the trial because he'd killed himself in jail in January that year. They sent her to Durham's Special Secure Unit, the official name for Hell Block.

I'd pleaded not guilty to laundering £1.6 million, carrying the cash across Europe in Lara's carrycot, but I wobbled on that plea when I was standing alone in the dock at Newcastle. Mum was only a few feet from me looking hurt, lost and terribly, terribly vulnerable. She was not yet fifty years old but she looked like a little old lady, all hunched up by her fears and confusion.

The prosecutor Anton Lodge QC liked his own voice. For him, Dad was 'The Godfather', the great Mafia Don. He started on about how Adele was shot aged seventeen and three months pregnant. The jury went 'Ooh.' I burst out crying and asked, 'What's that got to do with me?' I couldn't stop crying.

Mum was looking at eighteen months in prison for helping me with the bank accounts. That wasn't right. I couldn't risk her doing a day. The prosecution gave me a choice: plead guilty and the charges against Mum would be dropped. If I didn't, what would happen to Lara? Who would bring her up? They said the two words that convinced me to change my plea: Social Services.

I'd said nothing about anything or anyone in England or Italy. *Omertà*. If I had, I could have got a better deal. They had loads of paperwork evidence but it was just bank account details. If I'd shut the Geneva account and gone off with the cash, there wouldn't have been a paper trail. I didn't see myself as money laundering. Even though it was wrong, I didn't see anything I did as wrong at the time. When you're young it's exciting, you're on a power trip.

Now I faced the consequences.

If Mum stayed out of jail she could look after Lara. I had to plead guilty, and that's what I did on 23 November 1995. I don't remember leaving the dock when I was sentenced. There was only the echo: 'Marisa Merico, I sentence you to three years and nine months in prison. Take her down.'

The next I knew the sirens were wailing and we were racing across the Pennines. I was off to rejoin Myra and Rose and the rest of Britain's most dangerous women.

And to find love in different variations.

CHAPTER FIFTEEN
WHO'LL STOP THE RAIN?

'Love is stronger than justice'

STING,
TEN SUMMONERS' TALES, 1993

My court ordeal was over but prosecutor Maurizio Romanelli was still recounting the life and crimes of the Di Giovine and Serraino dynasties to magistrates in Milan. It was part of the Government's *Mani Pulite* [Clean Hands] legal showcase to trumpet the fact that they were acting against the Mafia. Dozens and dozens of trials went on for months and months. Some were held in a secure bunker courtroom, some televised, and all involved murder, drug trafficking, money laundering, gun-running and the one they could get everybody on – Mafia association. Almost all my family were up on one or more of those charges.

Auntie Rita was the star witness but at times the prosecutor had to deal with interruptions from the courtroom.

'Ugly whore!' Nan yelled out.

She was warned to keep quiet.

'But it's my daughter, your honour!'

Mum kept me in touch with the trials when she visited with Lara. Absolutely everybody who saw me had to get police security clearance. I learned the ways of Durham during my remand, but it was different being sentenced there. It was so final. When Mum and Lara left after the visits the pain was real. I could feel it and my whole body would shake. Heartbreak does hurt.

The things Mum had said all those years ago tumbled around in my head. What if I'd listened to her? What if? They were just words now. I had to do what I'd always done – accept my circumstances and deal with it. I'd be remorseful, I'd be sad and I'd be angry, but who was I going to shout at, who was I going to blame? The world? I got on with it.

Some days the atmosphere inside was thick with tension. My favourite fellow inmate Susan May helped ease it. She wrote formal letters for us prisoners, to MPs, lawyers and legal aid organisations, and everyone went to her, including Myra.

I asked, 'How can you sit in her cell and take notes?'

I think Sue's innocence meant she could see good in anybody. But I didn't understand it. She was from Oldham so she grew up with the horror of Myra Hindley. She could even have been one of her victims.

A lot of the reason I kept my head down in prison was because of Sue. I could have lost it but she held me back and spoke with the voice of reason.

Still, I couldn't have a bath because of Rose West. I saw her getting into it and no matter how much I scrubbed that bath I couldn't use it. She came over and sat down when I was having lunch with Sue once and I had to excuse myself. I said to Sue afterwards: 'If you know she's going to come, tell me because I don't want to sit with her. I'm not going to be horrible to her, but I'm not going to be nice to her.'

Yet Rose West looked like any other woman queuing up at Tesco. She didn't look evil. She wasn't hard-faced. She looked like a midwife or a nurse. She didn't look like a sexual monster.

That didn't help in the showers. Most of the girls covered themselves up and dried themselves discreetly. Not Rose West. She was quite blatant. She stood there naked in front of me. She had a black bushy forest on her. She wasn't a slim woman. She was just drying herself, patting herself off, and she looked at me and I freaked out a bit.

Myra was quite menacing. She had an aura about her. Girls would shout names at her but they could've saved their breath. She'd heard it all a million times. Myra was very thick-skinned. If you went past her cell it stank, a horrible overwhelming smell, a musky stale tobacco smell.

There was an IRA escape in 1995, after which security was tightened and we couldn't get our shopping at Sainsbury's any more, and they also segregated the Cat As on visits. It was all right for Rose West to be with everybody else, but not me. We were lepers and the screws sat at the table with us. Nothing was private. I couldn't stand being on visits with child killers around, especially with Lara there. I could cope with everything, but I couldn't cope with that. Yet I was in there with them. All because of money. And the money hadn't meant that much. The amounts were so vast – how high can you pile a million dollars? Rushing around Europe with all that money had been like playing Monopoly – and I got the 'Go to Jail' card.

I'd been in Hell Block for about eight months when I got friendly with Lisa Corah. From the age of twelve and through her teens she'd been abused by her sister's husband Philip and it had messed her up. Lisa found it hard to build a relationship but she started going out with a guy called Adrian. One night she told him about the abuse. He went mad. She begged him: 'Don't do anything. My sister has kids. She's family.'

Philip was a milkman and had just finished his round at 6 a.m. when Lisa's boyfriend put a pickaxe through his head, killing him sraight out. He ran off with the axe to Lisa's house saying, 'I've just killed him. What can I do with this?'

She was in shock. 'Just throw it over the back of the shed.'

It all kicked off and the police were trying to find out who the hell would want to murder a milkman. Lisa didn't say anything but they found the murder weapon at the back of the shed and she was implicated. She got life but on appeal it was knocked down to three years for aiding and abetting. Just for that one stupid mistake.

She was a good-looking girl, about twenty-two years old. I mentioned her on the phone to Naima and she asked, 'She's not a lesbian, is she?'

It had never occurred to me. 'No. She's not.'

Laughing, I mentioned this to Lisa later and she said, 'Actually, I am.'

I was quite naïve. We'd become really good friends and we used to train in the gym together, then one day she tried to kiss me. I'd never thought I would be attracted to a girl;

she was very attractive, very feminine, but she had a masculinity about her as well. She didn't wear make-up. She looked girly, but she used to wear rugby tops and shorts. I let her kiss me and I did find her attractive and things happened.

Afterwards I felt confused about my sexuality for a while but I decided, 'I'm in here and this is now and this is how I feel.'

I looked at Lisa as a person – not as a man or a woman, but someone that I cared for. Being with her I learned about myself and my body and what I want and what I don't want. I'm not ashamed of it. I don't see myself as bisexual. It was a love affair with a person in prison who happened to be a girl and it was a nice, special time in my life. We got through stuff together. We didn't go around holding hands or kissing. It was a loving, emotional uplift and cushion. I cared a lot about Lisa even though I wasn't 'in love' with her.

Four months after our affair began Lisa was released. I was upset because I was losing one of my best friends, apart from anything else, but I was happy for her. She kept coming to Durham to visit me for a while but then she met someone else on the outside. Part of me was gutted, and part of me wasn't bothered. I saw our love affair as something that happened in a set of circumstances that had now gone.

Then Frank came into my life.

Frank?

I could surely pick them. Frank Birley was one of the hardest men in the men's wing of Durham prison. And that's tough. He wasn't a saint. He was in Durham for the armed robbery of a Blackpool jeweller's. He wrote me a lovely letter. And he got Charles Bronson – not the late actor but the notorious convict – to draw cards and cartoons for me. Frank was one of the few who could keep Charlie Bronson under control. Famous for attacking prison officers, rooftop protests and taking hostages, Charlie is often referred to as the most violent prisoner in the UK prison system.

With money laundering the 'new' crime and with my international connections I was a good story and the newspapers were full of it: every time a Mafia trial in Italy hit the headlines I got fan mail. I got letters offering me this and that. Do you want a stereo? One offered me a canary. Then I got a letter from Frank: 'Hi, Marisa. I'm in the same situation as you. I'm a Category A prisoner. Hope you are all right in this country? Hope you are all right with the language. Hope you've got people looking after you. Wanted you to know I'm in the same boat. If you'd like to write to me ...'

I was always tagged 'Mafia' and with my name Frank obviously thought I was pure Italian.

I knew a couple of girls had got hooked up with relationships inside by writing to guys in the men's wing, but I always thought it was weird. How could you fall in love with a man you'd never met? I supposed it was fine if it kept them happy but I didn't think I could do such a thing. I'd always used Bruno as a good excuse to keep other men away. But with Frank I didn't do that. I wrote back thanking him for his letter: 'You sound like a really nice older guy. Thanks for your support.'

Next thing I got a letter in which he said he was only thirty. Oh! Then he sent a picture of himself. He played tennis in there and he had his tennis gear on. He was posing with his racquet. He was very fit. He was working out. He had curly dark hair. I remember I got the mail from the office, and going up the stairs I stopped and swore: 'My God. He's fucking gorgeous.'

I ran off to tell Sue. I'd got my knickers in a twist. The friendship started in 1996 and turned into more and more and more.

We would write A4, both sides, sheets and sheets, and send photographs. Every day, maybe twice or three times a day. We used to record our voices for each other. The guards listened to it, of course. Everything was vetted. Nothing went through without them hearing or seeing.

Then we started having little code words about stuff. Not anything bad. More on a personal level. I'd write a few Italian words and he would say, 'What does that mean?' I'd tell him what it was and he would write back with it. He asked me how to say 'I love you' in Italian and I told him and he began to say *'Ti amo'*.

I replied: 'You know, I think I love you too.'

It was intense. Everything was going into those letters. I do feel that I got to know him better through those letters than I would have in real life. It's easier to tell someone how you feel in a letter. At first I was cynical about the women who fell for men inside, but now it was happening to me.

Frank had a lot of money in there. He still had people on the outside doing stuff for him. His family looked after him. I never asked for anything but he sent me a box of books and gym gear and got his brother to send £1,000 in cash to me. I knew he'd be offended if I sent it back again. I knew men like him, like my dad, and I knew how their minds worked.

I wrote: 'I really appreciate this, but it's too much. I don't know when I can repay you.'

By return I got: 'Marisa, please do whatever you want with it. That is yours. I don't want it back. You're in there. You've had a hard time. You've had everything taken from you. If I can help, I will do that for you.'

I sent most of the money to Mum to help with looking after Lara, and he was happy about that. He was a genuinely loving man.

Which was in complete contrast to his prison record. He couldn't take the system and he protested in whatever jail he was in. He was involved in shit protests, when they smeared it all over the walls. He was hosed off in a roof protest at Preston. There was a segregation unit in Durham and he was always in that because he got pretty naughty there. In segregation they get locked up 24/7. You're not allowed out to socialise with other inmates. You can only go outside on your own.

Frank was in with the real tough guys. He was in the cage next to Charlie Bronson who, although he lives in his own little world, gets a lot of attention. But that'll happen if you kidnap prison governors. To him, these officers did wrong. Whatever they did, he didn't like them.

Frank had a tough life. His mum died when he was sixteen. His dad had been a Category A prisoner himself, a right villain, and Frank had followed in his footsteps. After the raid on the Blackpool jeweller's he ran off and the police cornered him. He went into a house and held a seventy-six-year-old woman and her daughter hostage in a nine-hour siege before being arrested. He wanted me not to dislike him for that and told me: 'It could have been a rugby team in there. I didn't know. I wasn't nasty to her.'

He wasn't. He made them cups of tea and looked after them. The women said he was a nice lad and the papers called him the 'Gentleman Robber'.

Frank did nine and a half years hard prison. A few times the screws beat him up badly. A rival prison gang ambushed him and scarred him. He had been through the wars.

In April 1996 my tariff in Durham was over. I was being released, set free, but Trevor Colebourne got wind that I might be re-arrested because Italy had a warrant for my arrest. The Italian authorities wanted me to face charges. At the *Mani Pulite* trials Mafia associates were being jailed for twenty years at a time. What would I get as a Di Giovine family member if was extradited to Milan? I might never see my daughter again. It was 50:50 that day.

Being released as a Cat A was unheard of; normally you are downgraded through the system before you go. Susan

May and the other girls were excited for me. The chief prison officer took me down to the gates after I'd gone through the release formalities. I was free for two steps.

I heard a helicopter as I was going out the gates of H Wing and thought, 'Oh shit. They're waiting for me. They're not going to let me go.'

The girls were at the windows shouting 'Bastards!'

There were snipers on the roof of the prison. There were gusts of wind from the copter blades as we walked out. Police cars were parked right by the gates.

A copper grabbed me and snarled, 'Are you Marisa Merico?

'Yes.'

He looked at the prison officer and asked, 'Is this her stuff?'

The officer nodded and he balled it all into the boot and bunged me in a police car and drove off with two escort bikes on the front, a car behind and the helicopter above us.

They took me to Durham police station and booked me in: 'You're arrested for extradition to Italy to answer charges of being involved in organised crime.'

It was all planned: two Scotland Yard extradition squad officers met me at Newcastle airport. I flew to Stansted airport and they took me into London to Charing Cross police station where I stayed overnight. I'd never felt freaked out in Durham and supposedly there are ghosts there. But in this cell I definitely felt there was somebody with me.

In the morning I woke up feeling a bit eerie but then 'Ordinary Day' by Duran Duran came on the radio. It had sad echoes for me. Michael, who'd been my first lover, had a brother called Chris who was my age. Chris took his own life when I was in Italy. He loved Duran Duran and they played 'Ordinary Day' at his funeral. I felt an overwhelming calmness when the song came on. I felt as if he was looking after me in some way. I know it sounds mad but I believe there must be something out there. I'm not sure if it is a God. I like to believe that there is something out there and once we go, our spirit doesn't.

I was remanded for three weeks at Bow Street Magistrates and taken to Holloway prison, where I became a new statistic, prison number TG0416. They couldn't cope at Holloway, they had no Cat A facilities. I kicked up about it, told them so. I should have shut up.

I got shunted back to Durham but not to my top-floor view of Durham Cathedral. I had a new cell. The security had tightened up so much that every month I had to go into a different cell. Each time I went in a cell, I had to clean it. It was an obsession, a touch of OCD, and I told them: 'You're moving me because you want me to scrub every cell in this place!'

The guards were terrified that the Mafia would break me out and fly me to freedom in a missile-equipped helicopter. We'd tried to do that with Dad in Portugal but I knew there was no possibility of it now because, apart from anything else, all my relatives were in jail – yet they acted on instructions that I was one of the most dangerous people in Britain.

I was back and forward to London, every time in an armoured vehicle, cuffed and shackled to my escort officer. Before I went out into the van I was strip-searched, following strict procedures so that I was never totally naked. Every time I went for a pee I had three guards outside the door. My every move was watched, and the claustrophobia was horrible.

I'd often be sick in the stuffy armed vans on the trips south but 'orders are orders' and they wouldn't open the cuffs to allow me to clean up. If I complained about anything I always got the same answer: it was being done, or couldn't be done 'for security reasons'. They seemed to think I was some comic-book super-villain, able to appear and vanish at will. The daughter of Arsène Lupin, indeed.

They'd stop for a break halfway through the five-hour journey. Often we stopped at Leicester prison, which is the local men's jail in the Southfields area. But once, for 'security reasons', we stopped at Leeds prison. At reception where they process the prisoners they told me there was a special toilet I could use exclusively. It had been built for a visit by Princess Anne. It was pink and frilly, very smart for a prison toilet. I got to use the royal facilities because I was a woman. The guards shackled me to a long chain and played it down the stairs to the toilet so I could just push the door to but I was still chained to them. I couldn't go anywhere else anyway. It was ridiculous.

They'd guard me in a cell as the escort guys took their tea break. I was an escape risk – no stopping at service stations.

They wouldn't stop anywhere but other prisons for, of course, security.

They told me they believed Dad was going to free me but Dad couldn't help himself at that time. My solicitor told me that somewhere in Whitehall it had been decided that I was to be treated as a Home Office prisoner, like an IRA terrorist. It was political. And everything to do with me was handled at high political level. The amount of money spent on me! They didn't have that sort of security with Rose West and Myra Hindley. God knows what they thought was going to happen. I wasn't going to leave my daughter anyway, no matter what, even if the cavalry came to get me.

After the stop at the royal loo, I was taken to Belmarsh prison, the Cat A men's jail in Greenwich where they bang up terrorists. I asked about Holloway but was told, 'They can't hold you there because they haven't got enough security.' They locked down the hospital wing and put me in a solitary cell. The woman officer told me, 'We've put a sheet over your window; don't go near it because if the men find out that you're a woman they'll keep you up all night.'

I was stripped-searched again but this time I had to strip off completely. They gave me a dressing gown and said: 'You need to squat.' I wasn't comfortable with that at all. It was horrible, demeaning. When I squatted, they put a metal detector underneath me.

I asked, 'What am I going to have in there. A gun?'

They just said they needed to do it.

When they left, I felt violated and very shocked. I shouldn't have been but I was. It upset me. I didn't feel very human or feminine. I knew I was just a name and number to them, but it didn't feel right. Of all the indignities I went through in the prison system that was the greatest. It made me wonder how on earth I had got to that moment, question every decision I had made. Was family loyalty, wanting to do what my dad wanted, to make him pleased with me, worth this humiliation? Just thinking about it makes me hurt with a deep, emotional damage. I was made to feel like a wild animal.

But the next time I appeared at Bow Street things were better. When I got back to Durham I told Susan May about the indignities of that first experience of Belmarsh. She wrote a letter, and my MP complained. The authorities admitted that what had happened to me was wrong. I'd made history as the first female to be held in a male prison. The next time I went I had the governor, the Samaritans and the priest at the door.

I'd got all that sorted, but by June 1996 I'd stopped going to Bow Street. Michael Howard, the Home Secretary, signed off on my extradition. I wouldn't see Lara. I wouldn't see Mum. What about my letters with Frank?

We kept writing because it took nearly eight months for the Italians to come and get me. A Scotland Yard extradition squad collected me to get on a plane on my twenty-seventh birthday, 19 February 1997. One of them was a big, tall bloke and nasty with it. His partner was quiet, but the tall bloke couldn't stop making snide comments, such as, 'They've put you in first class and I can't imagine why.' When they'd frog-marched me with armed police all around to the top of the stairs up to the plane he said: 'See you in fifteen years.'

His prediction might have been accurate but there was no need for that. I wasn't cheeky. I didn't swear at them. I just did as I was told. I didn't demand things. I was devastated because I'd left Lara, and I knew that I wouldn't see my little girl for ages. I'd already missed nearly three years of her life. She'd started school without me being there to take her to the school gates. She had new friends and her own interests. She was growing up without me.

When I was handed over to Italian Interpol my treatment all changed. The man and woman escort didn't worry about handcuffs on the plane. When the food came the woman asked: 'Would you like some wine?' I nearly fell off the seat. I hadn't had any wine for two and a half years. She was very kind. It was a different attitude altogether.

Especially when we landed in Rome. Two plainclothes cops took over and said they had to process me at Rome Central. One was quite flirty: 'Have you ever been to Rome before? We'll take you for a tour on the way.'

I saw the Coliseum on a beautiful sunny day in February. It was a real birthday treat after being lucky to get an hour a day in the open air at Durham. Later, they pointed out more sights as we drove to the north-east edge of the city, to Rebibbia, the location of Italy's major mixed penitentiary. We drove into Rebibbia prison through the Via Tiburtina entrance and I saw the churches of the Via Casal de' Pazzi and Piazza Ferriani. I wondered when I might ever see such beauty again.

In Rome the prison conditions were as convivial as the cops and the view, but it was only a couple of weeks until I was taken to Vigevano women's prison near Milan to await my trial.

My dad and Uncle Guglielmo had been extradited from Portugal, Bruno had been extradited from Spain. Nan and scores of others were already involved in the long trials in the special anti-terrorist, concrete-built courtrooms in Milan.

It was going to be a family reunion in court.

CHAPTER SIXTEEN
LA DOLCE VITA

In vino veritas
[In wine there is truth]

Nan and Auntie Angela had both been held at Vigevano and the inmates were very much aware of the Di Giovine name. I had a cell in the high-security wing; it had a sink, a toilet and a bidet but there was never hot water. I soaked my washing in the bidet and was getting ready to sleep one night when I thought I heard Bruno's sister Silvia's voice. It was, it *was* Lara's auntie.

I knew she'd been arrested. Guns connected to Bruno were found in her apartment. But I didn't know where she was after her eight-year conviction on arms charges. It was such a comfort to hear a friendly voice, someone I knew so well, that it gave me a warm glow. Maybe it was a good omen. We had lots of time to talk to each other, to speak about all that happened to everybody else in the extended families. Silvia and I poured our hearts out to each other. It was wonderful to be able to talk freely and not be concerned what I said. I was already a convicted felon, so what more could they do?

The prison had an association room where we'd cook for ourselves. They had a canteen and we'd make a list each week of things to buy. We were allowed two cartons of wine a day. It was prison paradise, the good life. Sometimes we'd save the cartons for a birthday blow-out and have a party. We'd ferment it with sugar and everybody would get smashed.

But I also got the girls fit. I was used to three hours a day in the Durham gym so I started aerobics classes in the yard. I'd get them stretching, doing handstands and cartwheels. We played volleyball in the gym once a week. I could release some of my anger when slamming the ball into the net. I did sit-ups in my cell. I did it all to help me sleep, to get my brain to switch off. If I didn't knock myself out with exercise, I'd just lie in bed worrying about the future, about Lara, and what would happen at my trial. Mum sent a parcel every week with Lara's drawings and tapes of her talking as well as loads of photographs. Such mementoes made me happy but terribly tearful at the same time.

And Frank was writing all the time. I'd thought our strange arrangement wouldn't survive when I left England, but it did. At first he had no idea where I was and phoned my mum, but she didn't even know I was in Rome. When it settled down we sent letters to each other every day.

It was November 1997 before I went to court in Milan for a mini-trial. Other family members had been dealt with in the previous weeks. Nan got life. *La Signora* had diabetes and was on a stretcher in court to hear the verdict, which made legal history – the only woman ever found guilty of such top-level Mafia association. She was carried from court by a team of *carabinieri* and was joking with them all the way. I wasn't there to see it but I bet she'd corrupted a couple before they even got her out of the courthouse.

Auntie Livia got twenty-four and a half years, which reflected her skill as an entrepreneur. Uncle Antonio and Uncle Filippo, who'd been with Dad in Spain and Portugal, got thirty years each. Grandpa Rosario, who was on a respirator during the trials, was serving eighteen years. Auntie Angela, born a month before me, got fourteen years. Uncle Franco had been hit with eight years at the start of the *Mani Puliti* trials in 1995. With the scores and scores of other Mafia associates, cousins and second cousins, friends and family, the total tariff before I got into the dock was near to 1,500 years.

Dad went off on a different trial. Italy had extradited him on drug trafficking charges but then charged him with murder. That broke the European extradition rules – you can't get a person back for one thing and charge them with another. It was all legal gobbledygook because he still got life in prison.

As did Bruno who, after spending three years in jail in Madrid, was done again in Milan on arms trafficking charges.

Uncle Guglielmo was in court with me. The 'Untouchable' prosecutor Maurizio Romanelli continually played back Auntie Rita's evidence: the details of the heroin deals, the movement of currency, the killings and control in the Piazza Prealpi. After we'd spent hours listening to this, Uncle Guglielmo turned to me and commented: 'Rita must have really hated you to say all that about you. God, she must have really hated you!'

I was devastated. I knew Rita was off her head with pills much of the time but she'd always been good to Bruno and me. I thought she loved me and helped me for that reason. I didn't need to hear this bile. Guglielmo was simply astonished at what she'd told them. And so was I.

Maurizio Romanelli told the court I was Dad's right hand, his voice, the financial wizard behind the money movement, the architect of the business operation. I should have known better. He picked out Angela and said that, unlike her, I hadn't grown up in the family. Angela grew up in that venal environment, and I didn't. Angela had got fourteen years – what would they do to me?

I was among the last to go on trial and Romanelli wanted more glory headlines. They were talking about twenty years. That was to frighten me. They gave me ten years. Lara would be sixteen when I got out. I'd be thirty-seven. I couldn't bear that thought so I changed my plea to guilty and was sentenced to six years. In that plea bargain I retrieved four years of my life.

That Christmas of 1997 I saw Lara for the first time in nine months. Mum put her on her passport and they came over for two weeks. I was allowed one two-hour visit a week so I had four hours with them altogether. It was wonderful and horrible at the same time. Kissing Lara goodbye was terrible because I didn't know when I'd see her again. They couldn't afford to keep visiting.

In January 1998 they gave me a release date of 2003. Frank was due out in 1999. I worried that he wouldn't wait around for me for four years. He hadn't even met me, for goodness sake!

Under Italian law you are not fully convicted until you have exhausted every appeal. I needed a last straw to hang on to and one of the family's lawyers, Vincenzo Minasi, found it. He discovered the Italians hadn't handled my extradition properly. When I was re-arrested outside the gates of Durham prison I should have been interrogated within five days by Maurizio Romanelli, the prosector. It didn't happen.

Minasi told me as only an Italian lawyer could, hands waving in the air: 'This is not right! We will not have this!'

And he didn't. Lo and behold, he got me out. It was Saturday, 13 June 1998, exactly four years and twelve days after I'd been arrested in 1994. The Italian legal teams had been going through Minasi's appeal and arguments and worked through to the weekend searching for rebuttal. I'd had so many knock-backs I thought it wouldn't happen, especially on a Saturday.

The senior officer that day at Vigevano was a nice lady; she was quite short and had a squeaky voice. The prison knew the appeal was in and she stayed with me in case I tried to kick off or even kill myself if the decision didn't go my way. It was a hot day.

'Di Giovine?' she said from my cell door.

I murmured something.

'Pack your stuff, you're going.'

I nearly passed out. I felt dizzy. My head was all over the place. I just remember sitting down hard on a chair and she said: 'Di Giovine? Are you okay?'

I burst into tears.

'Come on, Di Giovine. Get your stuff.'

I couldn't get out quick enough. I was in shock. All I had were a few items of clothing, some curtains and a gas burner – you had a gas burner in Italy so you could cook in your cell. I said goodbye to Silvia and gave her a kiss through the slot in the cell door. She started crying. For me, and for herself. I felt sorry for her and left her most of my stuff. I put the rest in a bin liner and walked down the corridor in the clothes I stood up in. The prison authorities gave me about twenty quid and that was it.

I walked out of Vigevano for the first time – I'd always been taken by armoured van before. Outside the gates there was a car park, and at the end of it there was a bus stop and a phone box. From there, I called Bruno and Silvia's mum. After she'd finished having hysterics, I said I'd meet her in the centre of Milan. I wanted a drink, and I wanted to get out of there. There was no shelter. There was no place I could get in the shade.

I got on the first bus that came along, carrying my bin liner, and the other passengers must have thought 'prison' but I didn't give a shit. I paid and I felt weird even doing that, having money. For four years I'd had no money in my hands. I'd used a pay phone but with a card, not money. There was nobody opening doors for me. Nobody. Four years. It's a long, long time. When you're on the outside it might not seem that, as the change happens gradually, day by day. I had to swallow it all in one hungry gulp. You know those flashbacks in the movies? For me it was the other way around but just as surreal. I'd stepped into the future.

I got off the bus near the train station and went into a nice, shaded café with a phone. Mum was at home. It was my friend Naima's wedding that day but she hadn't left yet.

'Mum, it's me. It's me, Mum. I'm out.'

I could hear the sigh of relief all those hundreds and hundreds of miles away. I talked to Lara for ages and then to Mum again. We babbled all sorts of arrangements. After that, all she wanted to do was get to the wedding and tell everybody, to share her happiness.

Frank had given me a number for his friend Barry and I called him with the news to pass on to Frank.

I took a moment to catch my breath at the café while I waited for Bruno's mum, listening to the rattle of cups and saucers and glasses clinking in the washing-up bowl, the squeal of the espresso machine and high-pitched voices – just another day in Milan. I'd survived prison in Italy and in England. I coped with it, got on with it. I thought then about Nan and Dad and all their brothers and sisters, the family on the Piazza Prealpi, how I'd started life in an environment where you had to be strong, had to stand your ground yet follow the rules. I realised I'd had private tuition that prepared me for years in prison. If you didn't fight your corner and give off a positive vibe you were stamped on, pushed out of the way. You got no respect. And that meant you got nowt.

I'd been stoic and strong and I was determined to stay that way to survive on the outside. Yet at first, leaving the institutionalised systems where your every moment is accounted for, I was a little lost. Bruno's mum and her brother took me back to her house. It was odd. I couldn't really eat, I was so emotional. I lost about half a stone in a week. Today I'd be ecstatic about that, but at the time I didn't really notice.

I was free, released on a technicality. My passport was in England with Customs and Excise. They had extradited me with no passport. Mum kicked up a fuss, got on to her MP and made a wonderful nuisance of herself. When Lara's school finished for the summer holidays she flew over on her own, escorted as an 'unassisted minor' on British Airways. She was with me for five weeks and it was lovely. We went away with Bruno's mum to the seaside, to Calabria, where once again I could take in the sweetness of the orange blossom, the aroma of the South.

But life behind bars was never far off. I visited Bruno every week once I got out, and I took Lara along to see him as well, but it was four years since we'd all been together as a family and we'd moved on. I was in love with Frank now. He couldn't phone me because he was Category A and was banned from making international calls but he was writing to me at my mother-in-law's house. Although that was awkward, I'd explained to her that I wasn't in love with her son any more. She knew the situation.

Lara went back to England for school just before her seventh birthday on 11 September. I was upset I was going to miss her birthday but I was still stuck in Milan. Mum had been berating Customs and Excise about my passport and eventually they got in touch with her old friend Roger Wilson, the guy who had had the frustrating job of interviewing her back when we were first arrested.

Mr Wilson probably, and quite happily, thought he'd heard the last of Patricia Di Giovine. He hadn't. He was brought into the whole confusing situation and at last they forwarded my passport to the British Embassy in Milan for personal collection. I picked it up on 16 September. I also got some cash – and itchy feet. There was nothing for me to hang around for. There was no point in having freedom if I couldn't be with my little girl.

On the same day Dad was involved in another mini-trial, charged with murder for the killing committed by the *Mafiosi* from the Camorra, the one he and Nan had sanctioned way back in 1988 when I had just moved over to Milan from England. The day I got my British passport back he was found guilty. I felt sick with the stress of it all. I was outside when they brought him from court and he smiled and waved. This time I blew him a goodbye kiss. I had no idea when I would ever see him again.

Bruno was in a different court later that day. He saw me and mouthed: 'Are you coming to visit me?' I shook my head. I saw the panic in his eyes because he knew I was going. He knew I was out, he knew Lara was in England, he knew what I was going to do. He had this horrible look of despair on his face. He was sad because he liked seeing me, but he wasn't my priority any more – neither was my dad. I thought they'd both had enough out of me. My daughter was number one in my life. And freedom, no matter how flimsy, was the only way I could be with her.

I was off. But not by plane. I couldn't afford the air fare. Bruno's mum drove me with my few belongings, a refugee's bundle, to Milan Central Station. I didn't get the sleeper on the night train, because that was too expensive. I looked like a student hitchhiker returning from the summer away. There was a young English couple in the compartment and I sat with them. At the Swiss border they just glanced at our passports and thought we were all together.

At Paris I changed trains and had a shower at the station. Time had moved on; before I went inside there were no public showers there. After we set sail from Calais I tried to phone Mum from the ferry but there was no answer. At Dover they glanced at my passport and that was it.

I was in England. And free in England. I looked around at the green fields and trees and they were all blurred by the tears in my eyes. I got on a train north, counting every minute until we reached our destination. I caught a taxi from the station to Mum's house and rang the bell.

'Who is it?' she called.

'Father Christmas,' I replied.

But I was the one getting the present. Lara came running to the door and gave me a huge hug, and that was the only gift I ever wanted. I couldn't stop staring at her as she showed me all her favourite toys and clothes and chatted about her friends and what they were doing at school. That night I sat and watched her for ages after she went to sleep. I couldn't get enough of just looking at her.

The next day I got some funny looks when I took her to school. It had been in the papers that I was freed in Italy. Someone told Radio Lancashire I was home and the local papers wrote about me. Hordes of journalists were on the doorstep but I said nothing to them.

They wrote their so-called 'interviews' anyway. One guy reported in the *Sunday Mirror* that I had a nice bum so I didn't complain about the quotes he used that I hadn't given. I wasn't interested. I hadn't said more than a couple of sentences publicly until I decided to clear the air and tell the true story with this book.

But I talked to Frank.

I'd never heard his voice 'live', only on the tapes he sent me. He was in Hull prison and got permission to ring me at Mum's house. It was weird and awkward. But wonderful. There was kismet about it. I'd been arrested on 1 June 1994 and he was arrested on 1 June 1990, for the raid on the Blackpool jeweller's.

He said he wanted me to visit but as he was a Cat A I had to be vetted, and I wouldn't easily get a visiting order. I wasn't in hiding. The UK authorities knew I was back. I had no money because all my assets, including my house, had been seized. I was on benefits, I'd applied for and been given a council house. I was in the system. The Italians were the only people who could make trouble because I'd served my time in England. I took the risk and applied for vetting.

Frank told me he was going to court again for breaking a prison guard's jaw. The first time I saw him in person he was behind a bulletproof screen. I met his family, his brother John and his dad's wife Debbie, in Leeds and went to the Hull court with them. Frank looked around the court and we locked eyes. It was the first time we'd ever seen each other in the flesh. He looked tired but nice, although I'm sure the warder who'd had to have his jaw pinned back together wouldn't agree. Frank did it but was found not guilty as there was no evidence.

It was November before I was given clearance to visit. By this stage he was in maximum security at Whitemoor prison in Cambridgeshire. As a Cat A he was segregated in a closed-in area with a special officer on guard. When I first saw him, he was shaking with nerves and I was nervous as well. He looked pale and he'd lost some weight. He gave me a hug and a kiss. Not a proper kiss – we were still getting to know each other – but I could smell his skin, and I liked the smell.

I was wearing a figure-hugging chocolate knitted dress. I'd gone on a sunbed before the visit. My hair was long and blonde and nearly to my bum. I tried to make the most of what I had available.

We talked and talked, not about anything important, but just because we could talk to each other without a tape. We kissed at the end of the visit and that's when it began. I went to see Frank every week after that. He'd act up and be moved from one place to another. He used to hate the young officers coming in and telling him what to do with no respect, so he'd kick off. They put him in jail all over England, in with nonces, with the sex offenders, and down in the cages, with the highest security possible. The only place he didn't go was Parkhurst on the Isle of Wight – but he'd been there in the past. Wherever, whenever there was trouble, Frank's name would be on it. They hated him in that system. They absolutely hated him. He was almost as notorious as Charlie Bronson.

When he wasn't kicking off, he was writing to me or phoning me. We carried on like that until 15 October 1999, a Friday morning, when he was released from Doncaster prison. He wanted me to go and pick him up at 7 a.m. I'd bought him a rose but I accidentally left home without it and had to turn back and then I was behind schedule. When I got to the prison Frank was waiting outside in the cold in only a white T-shirt and trousers. I couldn't believe it. I didn't watch him come out. *He* was waiting for *me*! I felt terrible. I gave him a hug and a kiss and said sorry to be late:

'I went back to get your rose,' I explained.

He was laughing. He always had a quiet smile, a twinkle in his eye that told you when he was happy. This morning it was as if he'd showered in glee. I didn't think anyone could grin that much. He opened the boot of the car to put his stuff in and there was a big bunch of flowers for me. He'd got his cousin Dennis to buy them and hide them in my boot!

It was only 8 a.m. and I drove to a motorway service station where there was a hotel and café. He tucked into his first 'free' full English breakfast in years. We looked at each other, took photographs, hugged and kissed, but that was as far as it went. Later he told me: 'I was dying to take you into that hotel, but I felt it was too cheeky.'

I wanted him as well but my period had come on the night before, which was a blow. I knew I wanted to have a baby with Frank – I'd come off the Pill with that in mind – but for that morning I had to put seduction out of my mind. It was sexual stalemate.

On the drive to my home we stopped at his brother's in Leeds. John had bought him a whole new wardrobe, nice tops and jeans, and he gave him £2,000. And then friends and relatives arrived to give him a big homecoming welcome, which made him feel overwhelmed.

He dozed and talked on the drive to Blackpool and my council flat in Poulton. On the Saturday we got up late and, like a little boy, he wanted to go to a toy shop. He bought Lara loads of stuff and then got himself a remote control car, an American Warrior Wagon that cost a couple of hundred quid. It seemed this armed robber was just a big kid.

When we talked about having a child together, he said he'd always wanted to become a dad but thought it wouldn't happen. He'd had a girlfriend Nicola for a long time before he went inside and they left it to nature but she never got pregnant. He thought it was him. I said we'd see what happened, and the very first month he was home I got pregnant. Frank told everybody instantly – exactly what you don't do. Three days after the positive test I started bleeding as though I had a really bad period. It was a miscarriage. I was distraught and Frank was as well, but the doctor said there was no reason not to try again.

Anyway, we were a family with Lara. Frank began spending four days a week with us and the rest of the time over in Leeds. All his friends and family were there. He liked going to a café at Roundhay Park, and once the DJ Jimmy Savile walked in, all loud and cigar smoke. Frank and his mates were sitting chatting and Jimmy Savile looked around and asked, 'All right, the Leeds Mafia. Are the gangsters in?'

Little did he realise that they were. Frank replied, 'If you want to keep running your marathons, Jimmy, you'd better sit down and shut up.'

Apparently, Jimmy Savile went a little pale and did both.

The problem was that Frank had come out to a lot of gang tensions and rivalry. When he went into prison he'd had a partner called Mark McCall who completely dropped him and didn't help while he was inside. Frank could have grassed him up but he didn't, and Mark made a lot of money. When Frank got out, Mark wasn't happy about him coming back to Leeds. Frank wanted to go it alone, and have nothing to do with Mark. He told him: 'I've let you be for nine years. You've made your money, you never bothered with me. You never bothered with my family. You haven't looked after me, nothing. I'm out now. I'm trying to get on with it. You leave me alone, I'll leave you alone.'

It didn't happen that way, though. The situation started getting heated. I knew things weren't good when Frank started wearing a bullet-proof vest. It was a wake-up call for me. Did I really want to be involved in the gangster lifestyle again and risk getting caught up in crime myself? I couldn't face getting caught and being taken away from Lara. I'd said to Frank in our letters in prison, 'I don't want to get involved in anything like that again. I don't care if we live on a rubber dingy at the end of the pier, I don't want that life.' And I meant it. I had to keep my nose clean now.

On my thirtieth birthday, in February 2000, we were planning to see a movie rom-com called *The Love Letter* and then have dinner. I was getting ready when Frank telephoned.

'Right, we're going to Birmingham.'

'You what? I thought we were going to the cinema.'

His sighed: 'Do you wanna go to the cinema? Or do you want to go and pick up twenty-eight grand?'

We went to Birmingham.

CHAPTER SEVENTEEN
MEAN STREETS

'You can close your eyes to the things you do not want to see, but you cannot close your heart to the things you do not want to feel.'

GIUSEPPE GARIBALDI, 1832

As we drove down the M6 to Birmingham, Frank explained the story behind the cash he was going to collect. Frank's great friend and partner, who I'll call Nad, a big, lovable rascal of a lad, had been approached by a couple of Frank's former associates. They wanted to do a drug deal and to cut Frank out. Nad didn't kick off when they made the offer. He went along with it. They paid him £60,000 for a delivery of cocaine that never existed. He then gave them the finger and split the money, minus £2,000 in expenses, with Frank.

Nad was powerful enough to get away with it. He told them it was a lesson: 'You deserve it. Nobody goes behind Frank's back.'

We met Nad briefly and collected the money in a blue, zip-up gym bag. Afterwards, Frank said, 'Right, we're not travelling back up in that car. Wipe it clean, we'll ditch it.'

We did, and grabbed a taxi back to Blackpool, at a cost of £150. Frank rounded it up to £200 with a tip. He had the cash and as far as I could see he hadn't broken the law per se. All we were doing was collecting cash that was due to him. It was nothing to do with me. The worst that could have happened if we were stopped by the police would be that the money was confiscated. I wasn't taking any risks myself.

With the cash under the bed, I booked a holiday to Fuerteventura in the Canary Islands. It wasn't that brilliant but it didn't matter; we just wanted to relax and escape the aggro that was building up around Frank. We had lots of sun and sex and I got pregnant again. I'd bought about half a dozen pregnancy test kits and I left them lying in the bathroom. He came in and sat on the edge of the toilet seat and looked at it then he shook his head: 'I don't think I'm ever going to be a father.'

I smiled. 'Of course, you will. I'm pregnant.'

He still didn't get it. I showed him my boobs, which were hard, the veins standing out. 'That's a sign, proof. I am.'

He was fantastically happy, but prospective fatherhood didn't stop him getting up to no good. He wanted to get into the nightclub business and needed a lot of funds. He thought if he invested in this, he'd get that, and finally he'd have enough. Money he'd given for others to invest had vanished in schemes that had gone wrong. It put him in a corner.

'Marisa,' he said, 'I've got to do something to try and get some cash to make it legitimately. I'll do that and then stop.'

He went to Holland to organise a drugs deal and it was arranged I'd pick him up in our BMW convertible when he returned to Leeds. I just had time to do that and get back to collect Lara from school. Frank was asleep in the car as we got to a roundabout. I saw a police car and then another and another pulling up behind us. There were cars ahead of us as well.

'Frank! Frank!' I started nudging him. 'Wake up. There's too many police here.'

As I shouted at him a Vauxhall Vectra flashed its lights in front of us. We were being ordered to pull up. It was awkward because as you come off that motorway junction there's nowhere to park. The cop cars stopped us at the worst possible spot and stopped the traffic either way on this busy highway. The queues lengthened as we sat in our car. People were staring, slowing down more to have a good gawp.

The police wanted our documentation, then said they were going to search the car.

Frank said: 'For God's sake. You know who I am. I've just done nine years. You really think I'm going to have something in my car? You're not going to find what you want in there.'

But they found lots of goodies. A hat in a huge box for me. And sex toys from Holland – a maid's outfit and crotchless knickers and body stockings.

I was in hysterics and told Frank, 'I'm not wearing that! You kinky sod.'

He was laughing but embarrassed.

The coppers were *angry* and embarrassed – there wasn't anything they could get us on. We were both recent Cat A prisoners, held at Her Majesty's pleasure. Surely there had to be more than sex toys in the boot? But there wasn't. They said we had to show up at Poulton Station with our driving licences and insurance and let us go.

Frank was a free man. There were no conditions on his release and he could go anywhere he wanted. Clearly he was being watched, though. The police had been tipped off and knew he'd been to Holland. They believed he was arranging a drug deal and they were right. He'd met up with Mr Big and negotiated a profitable exchange. But the Dutch deal went down the drain because his ex-partner Mark McCall put a spanner in the works and bad-mouthed Frank to the guy in Holland, who called it all off. That made Frank very mad. Things were happening. I wasn't very happy. I was pregnant, after all.

One night, one of Frank's friends, Craig Mirfield, who was only in his twenties, was gunned down. He was shot by a bullet that was meant for Frank. Craig, who had three children, was part of Frank's gang.

There was another gangster in Leeds apart from Mark McCall who didn't like Frank and wanted him out of the way. He threatened what they had. They were greedy and didn't want to share. They were fearful of Frank's reputation as he was a lot stronger than them. They were deadly enemies in the middle of an already-escalating drugs war on the streets of the Yorkshire city. And they sent someone to find Frank and kill him. The shooter found Craig instead. The gunman was coked out of his head and targeted the wrong vehicle. He jumped out in front of Craig's van and shot him through the windscreen. Craig died instantly.

Frank felt absolutely awful that this lad had been shot because of him and he gave most of the £28,000 to Craig's family. I was very upset about the whole situation but I wasn't going to leave Frank. He was my man. But it was tough knowing the danger he was in, and worrying about the problems it could cause for us all.

In March 2000 one of my Italian family was released from jail on a technicality. A false passport was never a family problem and he travelled over to England. My relative still had contacts in Spain and onwards with the man known only as 'The Sultan' in Morocco. He thought so much of me he offered Frank an unprecedented deal. He would get them to supply hashish and Frank would only have to pay *after* he marketed it. The suppliers trusted my family so much they would deliver the drugs with nothing upfront. That was a massive gesture. Nobody else would do that.

If Frank had to mess about, go illegal, this was a more protected option. I only encouraged it because I so desperately wanted Frank to get away from the madness going on with the Yorkshire gangsters. We'd heard they'd put a price on Frank's head, just as had happened to my dad.

It reminded me of the Mafia wars I'd witnessed, armed men in territorial battles. I pleaded: 'Look, if you've got to do something, why do it in Leeds? Who cares? They're all idiots. They are nobodies. You could be better than them if you wanted to.'

Frank dug his heels in. He had to prove a point. When they killed that lad, Frank went off the rails. He completely lost it, didn't care any more. I was upset because we had a baby coming and I'd thought we'd be able to move away from all this, to have a new life, a family life.

All he would say when I saw him was: 'I'll be fine, I'll be fine.' He was distant with me and I knew he was wheeling and dealing and up to stuff he wouldn't talk about.

It was the Easter holidays 2000 and we were going to spend the weekend in Leeds at the De Vere Oulton Hall Hotel. It was to be a romantic getaway, all posh and candlelight. I was nearly three months pregnant. School was out and Lara had flown to Italy to stay with her grandma, Bruno's mum, and to go with her to visit her dad in jail.

It was Friday evening. Frank was coming back home and we were going to drive across to the hotel together the next day.

He rang me about 8 p.m. and said, *'Ti amo.'*

'Are you all right? Are you coming home?'

'I'm not sure.'

'Try and come home. I want to see you. I miss you.'

'Right. Right. Right.'

I watched television, but he didn't appear. I rang him about 11.30 p.m. and the mobile kept ringing. I went to bed but woke up with a start at 1 a.m. and called him again. Still no answer.

What's happened? What was he doing? He wouldn't usually do this. He would let me know what he was doing. I fell back asleep and next morning I phoned his brother John, angry and worried: John where is he? What's going on with him? He could be dead in a ditch for all I know.'

'Marisa, don't worry. I booked him a hotel room last night. He was either going to use it or not. I'll go and find out.'

I called Nad but he was in Birmingham and thought Frank had come home to me.

I was getting angrier with Frank for messing me around but at noon John called: 'I can't find him. Get yourself across here.'

We had a massive Mitsubishi 4x4 but I didn't want to take it on the motorways so I took the back roads. I had just reached Preston when the phone rang. It was an Irish friend of Frank's: 'Marisa, I'm so, so sorry to hear about Frank.'

'What you do mean? What have you heard?'

'Oh!' He paused, surprised. 'Oh.'

'I think you'd better tell me now. What are you talking about?'

'He got shot last night.'

I felt dizzy. I felt sick. I burst out crying.

'What are you saying?'

'Well, Frankie got shot last night.'

'I've got to ring John. I've got to ring John.'

I rang John: 'He's telling me that Frank got shot last night. What is going on?'

'He doesn't know what he's on about, he's an idiot. Just get yourself across here.'

I was driving with tears streaming from my eyes, and half of me was thinking, 'Maybe he's got it wrong,' but the other half was in shock. I don't know how I drove there but somehow I got to John's. As I was getting out of the car John walked over, his face red and his eyes raw. Raw, red raw.

I kept thinking in my head: 'No. No. No.'

He came to the car door: 'Marisa. I'm so sorry. I'm so sorry.'

There were others around and they grabbed hold of my arms and sort of frog-marched me into the house. I collapsed on the settee crying and crying and crying. I thought my heart had been cut out. They were all in shock but trying to help me because I was carrying his baby. I was the most vulnerable at that moment.

Frank's sisters and several other people arrived. A police family liaison officer was there, and everybody was uncomfortable because they didn't want her around. She wasn't much help anyway.

I broke down: 'I'm never going to wash his clothes again. I'm never going to cook for him. Oh my God. He's never going to see our baby. He *knew*. He *knew* he'd never be a father.'

That fatal Friday, Frank and a younger lad had gone to the home of one of his enemies, a grand palace of a place with big security gates. And guards. They had gone to put the frighteners on the gangster trying to intimidate Frank. One of the reports said they were on a 'punishment raid'. Nobody will ever know exactly what Frank's intentions were that night in April 2000. There were many demons, real or imagined, unsettling him. He was a tormented soul.

It was pitch black and a man appeared in the grounds, a seventeen-year-old who looked much older. A single shot blasted off at him. It caught the teenager in the leg. All hell broke loose, lights and alarms and shouting.

Frank and his mate sprinted through the gardens and up to a six-foot-high fence. Behind it was a walkway, a tight squeeze between a caravan and a garage. Frank told the lad to watch him climbing over and then follow. At his back, the lad got over the fence with the gun in his hand.

He jumped down with the gun and a shot went off. The fatal shot.

Did this lad aim and shoot to kill Frank?

Frank had a lot of enemies who wanted him out of the way at any cost.

Was it an accident? The gun had apparently jammed the day before. So was it dodgy? It's still a big question mark for me.

With whatever intention the bullet was fired, it struck Frank right in the back of his neck. Above his protective clothing. More questions. A freak shot? The work of a sharp-shooter?

Frank got up, staggered a few steps down the road and fell to the ground. He cried to the lad: 'Help me!' But the lad ran off. An ambulance took Frank to Leeds Royal Infirmary where he died at 1.15 a.m. That's the time I woke up at home. When I startled myself awake, I swear to God, I had this weird feeling that Frank was there with me.

The lad ran off and has never been caught. No one has ever been done for Frank's death. John, Frank's brother, had a chat with the lad. He was very upset about it all and said that ten minutes before it all happened Frank had been saying, 'I'm so happy. My girlfriend is having a baby, and life is wonderful.' He swore it was an accident and John and Frank's father let it go at that.

The police never arrested anybody. Frank's death is in some computer file now. The night he died a few of the policemen in Leeds went out for a drink to celebrate.

When I drove home after Frank died I felt my whole life crumbling. We'd been together outside for just six months but it was such a serious relationship. Psychologically, I'd taken a kicking, and I knew our unborn child would soon be kicking too.

There were a few of the split-seconds we all have in our lives when I thought it might be better for the world if I was out of it – but I had Lara to pull me back from that silly idea.

I always believed in survival. I'd never give up.

Now I had a little bundle inside me letting me know the fight for life was still on.

CHAPTER EIGHTEEN
BORN AGAIN

'Farewell to the monsters, farewell to the saints
Farewell to pride.
All that is left is men.'

JEAN PAUL SARTRE,
THE DEVIL AND THE GOOD LORD, 1951

I screamed out all the pain of Frank's death and the anguish of the weeks that followed it at the Royal Victoria Hospital in Blackpool on 21 October 2000. My waters had broken and I refused any anaesthetic when our baby started arriving. Little Frank took six hours to be delivered and we did it together on gas and air, the most natural way. I needed to feel the pain as he was born. I called him Frank for I wanted him to know about his dad, who was not perfect but had a side that was good and kind and loving.

His dad's funeral in Leeds had been difficult. There were lots of people, some of them strangers to me, even members of his extended family. It was a day in the twilight zone.

Some folk had put flowers at the post where Frank fell when he was shot. A few of the messages talked about the 1990 American film *King of New York* in which Christopher Walken plays a big-time gangster who gets out of jail and pursues a vendetta against his criminal competition. So that's what they thought.

With young Frank and Lara to worry about, I turned my thoughts away from the underworld power struggles in the north-west of England to my own extended family at home, in Italy and beyond. I was the one on the outside trying to watch out for the interests of an astonishing assortment of characters and deal with the continuing Mafia machinations.

Valeria Vrba, the glamorous and determined survivor, was living in Slovakia with her daughters Etienne and Giselle, who was my sister. She'd escaped the authorities but was very much a wanted woman because, along with me, Valeria was important in the movement of our money around Europe, Holland, Switzerland, Germany and Spain. Valeria had corrupted several women in the banks in Geneva and Zurich and those women had testified against her to save themselves some years in jail.

There was a lot of money in those accounts and I would love to know who kept it. Did it go into somebody's pocket? Wherever it went, Valeria was in the frame for laundering millions in a string of currencies.

When I talked to her from Blackpool, I advised her to get a lawyer to sort out her situation but she said it would be too expensive. Only half a dozen or so years earlier I'd have given her the money without batting an eyelid but now I simply didn't have it. I told her she should get out of Slovakia and go to a country where she would be safe from extradition but she didn't listen to my warning. She was sending Etienne once a year to visit her father, Mario the Sicilian, in Brazil unaware that he still wanted revenge on her and my father. He had waited and waited for the most hurtful and, for him, the most perfect time. In 2000 he found out that Etienne was flying out of Vienna Airport and that Valeria would be there to see her off. She could have sent her brother or someone else but it was only about an hour's drive across the border from her home and she wanted to see her daughter off safely.

She was arrested by the Austrian police acting for Interpol after Mario described her exact movements for them. Etienne flew to Brazil and has never returned. No one has heard from her or anything about her ever since. Valeria was extradited to Italy, leaving six-year-old Giselle with her grandma, just as I had had to leave Lara with my mum.

There were a few months when no one knew where Valeria was. I couldn't get hold of her and I didn't know what the hell had happened to her. Eventually Dad found out on the prison grapevine that they'd thrown the book at Valeria. They had it all in taped conversations between her and Swiss women bankers. She was jailed for eighteen years.

So Giselle was one of the increasing number of people I had to worry about. Mum had suffered a lot with her health and had to have heart surgery. She was still able to help me with babysitting and school runs but we were finding it a struggle to live on the little money we had coming in. I tried to get jobs, even stacking shelves in the supermarket, but with my criminal legend I never got any employment. There's not a lot of call for Cat As.

What concerned me most was a knock on the door from the Italian authorities. Would what happened to Valeria happen to me? Would they ever extradite me? And if so, what would happen to Frank and Lara?

Nan was diagnosed with terminal cancer in 2007, a life sentence that ended the one imposed by the state. She was freed under a supervision programme and now lives back on the Piazza Prealpi. Life has come full circle for her. But Grandpa Rosario is no longer around. He became so ill during the trials that he had to stop attending and he died in 1999.

As she was throughout their marriage, Nan remained the more powerful figure. Even she can't beat cancer but she's stared it in the eye and slowed it down, delayed the inevitable. She's still finding ways around the system – any system they throw at her.

Uncle Guglielmo is out of jail and has a new life in Spain with his new wife and their two sons. Auntie Angela is married and has a son, and she also looks after Nan in Milan.

Dad was also released in 2007 but into even stricter supervision. Again he's one of the most wanted men in the world – by the Mafia this time. He's in the Italian witness protection programme. He testified at a number of trials, giving evidence for the prosecution against families just like the Di Giovine–Serraino clans. It was high risk and there has been flak from the families, especially the Calabrian clan.

When Dad got arrested, none of the family in the South helped him. They were all out making their own money and not one of them said anything to him. I believe that's why Dad did what he did. He got so fed up with them that he made a deal to get himself an element of freedom in the witness protection system. He was helped in this by Dottore

Macri Vincenzo, who is a major player in the anti-Mafia brigade in Rome.

No one in the world knows where Dad is now. I speak to him on the phone but the sources of calls are shielded to keep him safe. He is very estranged from everything and everyone from the past. He knows so much: he's been in the Mafia for more than half a century and dealt with underworld figures, arms dealers and major drug traffickers on a global scale. Now, he says, at last there's a decent price on his head.

I don't know if Nan's release was anything to do with Dad's arrangements with the Italian government but she still keeps in touch with the family in the South. It's taken time but she seems to understand why Dad did what he did. But in 2009 it got a little crazy because he had to testify in a trial involving the next generation of Nan's Calabrian family. They are still cousins and quite close. Dad's evidence was bad for the family and they went mad. Nan was really angry with Dad and wouldn't speak to him for a couple of months. Later, she told him: 'I know what you're doing, but you don't have to get so personal.'

He didn't want to go against the family but he had no choice. They were as much embarrassed as angered by it. It wasn't good for their status. They're still doing what they are doing. They're still the Mafia. They're still in business.

Dad has shocked a lot of people. I asked him about it towards the end of 2009 and he told me: 'I cannot live with myself in thinking that I was part of that scum. They are all scum. They've got no respect. They've got no sense of honour. They are no longer men of honour. I don't remember going out and hurting old people. I don't remember, because I never did it. Now there is just too much dirt. It's like the lowest of the low. It's not like old school, it's not like it used to be.'

I know what he means. It's these jumped-up young ones who think they can do whatever they want. It doesn't matter what reputation anybody else has, they think they're better. They think they know more.

And Europe is now a melting pot of gangsters, with the influx of Albanians and other nationalities, especially on the streets of Milan. They don't have rules and they don't have respect, as my family in Milan is constantly finding out.

Dad has done wrong in his life but things were never as bad as they are now in the 21st century when young kids are being shot in the street. We live in a world of what I call 'plastic gangsters'. They're not real and they don't know what is.

Dad met many underworld figures in Europe and America. Lots of them met violent ends, including his Italian-American connection Paul Castellano, whose murder was ordered by 'Dapper Don' Gotti on 16 December 1985.

Dad and I have talked about a lot of things, but obviously it's on the phone so it's different. I can never look into his eyes and judge what he's saying. Yet I have more of an understanding of him now, and he has of me. He's got a lot of regrets. He used to think he could buy my affection but that always got on my nerves. All I ever wanted was his time – but he spent his time gallivanting with women and that was his priority. Work and women. He was chasing dreams and ideas. The time he spent with me wasn't proper time. He took me for granted. He used to spend more time with Anna Marie, the child he had with Fanny in New York when he was posing as Count Marco Carraciolo. In a strange twist of fate, in 2009 she had a DNA test and it turns out she wasn't Dad's daughter after all. How ironic that Dad spent more day-to-day time with her than he'd ever done with me.

He says now: 'I regret not being with you more. I can't go back in time, I wish I could. My biggest dream was always to make a palace for us all, to have all the family together. I just kept going to get more money to set it all up.'

There never was one big, last job. That's all academic now.

Maybe I'll never be able to sit down and talk to him face to face again. I never know when he might call and I have no way of contacting him. He's very much a secret weapon.

Auntie Rita's evidence was the fatal flick that brought down the house of cards. She left the witness protection programme in 2008. I still feel uncomfortable with it; to me what she did was the ultimate betrayal of her immediate family. I could never understand that. That was part of the life she was born into.

Just as I was.

I know terrible things have been done. I regret the fact that I have ever hurt people indirectly: the people who took the drugs and died; the guns that I sat on that may have gone on to kill. I regret that with all my heart and I'm still paying for it now.

I don't regret having had a certain lifestyle where I saw a lot of things and got to do a lot of things. I wouldn't have that otherwise. I was being treated as a Mafia Princess, having money, going to buy what I wanted, when I wanted. I don't regret that. I've paid for that.

I hated every minute I was in prison, even though I met some great people in there and had some experiences that made me a lot stronger. Because of that, I am the person that I am today. It's made me more humble, more compassionate, more understanding of others. I don't judge on first sight any more. There's always something behind a face. You can't tell by looking if someone's a saint or a monster. Often, they don't know themselves. And that's terrifying.

CHAPTER NINETEEN
FAMILY VALUES

'I'll make him an offer he can't refuse.'

MARLON BRANDO AS DON CORLEONE,

THE GODFATHER, 1972

We held my beloved daughter Lara's eighteenth birthday party at a social club near our home in Blackpool on 11 September 2009. She's her own woman now. Reaching the age of maturity gives her the freedom to make her own choices, and her own opportunities. I believe turning eighteen is the transition to being an adult. In charge of your own life. It was for me and for my mum. We made our decisions, took our journeys.

I don't worry about Lara falling in love with an Italian and going out to live there, as we did, because she could just as easily meet someone bad round the corner in Lancashire. You can't think like that. She's a strong-minded girl but she knows how life can go wrong and I think she's smart enough not to make the mistakes I did.

Lara has been to visit her dad every year that he's been in jail but always with my mum or Bruno's mum. And always in prison. In August 2009 she thought she'd see her dad on the outside for the first time. Bruno was released after serving seventeen years on the arms and drugs charges. He was out, pending an appeal against that very release.

I made arrangements for Lara to go and see him and, now that he was free, to take her little brother Frank to visit too. It was all set, the flights were booked, when Bruno was re-arrested. We got the news while my sister Giselle was over visiting us from Slovakia. She's half my age and hasn't seen her mum since she was arrested. At least Lara saw Bruno regularly even if it was during prison visits. Sadly, they were not together on their shared birthday. They never have been.

Lara speaks and understands Italian very well but I'm only told that, for she never uses it in front of me. She's got that silly teenage shyness about speaking a foreign language in front of me or her mates. Her dad says she chatters away perfectly well to him.

She's got a boyfriend – he's English. A nice lad, who's handy at helping to put up shelves in my kitchen. He was at her party along with some other friends her age but I wanted as many family members there as possible. Frank's folks from Leeds came over and there were my English aunties and mum, of course, chatting away. She worries more about the plot of *Coronation Street* on the telly now than the Mafia. Most of the Italian family were unable to attend Lara's eighteenth, unavoidably detained.

Since Frank's death I've only had one serious love affair and that had its complications. I bring a lot of history with me but also, for the right person, my passionate love and loyalty. Now I would have to be in a full partnership; I could no longer act to order or to please. I want to act with a man as a unit, move together with a purpose towards a future.

I legally separated from and then divorced Bruno; the paperwork was finally completed in 2000 when I got back to England, because there was no future for us. Life changed for me in many ways when I came to England; I knew I couldn't have a gun under the tiles, or hide money any more. In Italy you could, and you could behave in a certain way. That's how it was. I think in Italian when I speak the language, and it's the same with English.

I have never said I was innocent because I'm not. I'm not an angel. I'm not a devil. I'm in between. I've done wrong, and I sat in prison for more than four years. I've paid for it. I didn't in any shape or form try to get out of it, even though I was very young and very naïve when I became a Mafia Princess. It's different now; I'm more aware of what's going on in my surroundings.

I am loyal literally to the death. I'm like that with my friends. People don't stick to their values or their principles. Or to their loyalty. I do. This is what has got me into trouble – the loyalty I have felt towards my own blood. People that I cared about and loved. It's got me into trouble because it's in my blood, part of what and who I am.

I want a life of stability and happiness now. There will always be stress – you can't eradicate the past – but let's hope it will continue to be about who's taking the cat to the vet for his shots. Or if Lara will catch the last bus. Or is the new *Terminator* movie going to spook little Frank, who is not quite nine years old? He likes all these films and video war games. I watch him blasting away and think of his dad.

After one games session he asked me, 'How do you get killed with one bullet?'

His dad was. Killed with one bullet. Which is something else I am going to have to go into with him. My son is growing up and one day he will want to know what happened. I wouldn't want him to take it into his own hands to get revenge, maybe bring on a vendetta. I'm worried that when he's eighteen or nineteen years old, more full of more testosterone than thought, he might go looking for his dad's killer. And because of that horror scenario, I have always quietly kept in touch with people who might know the answers. One man whom I have respect for told me not to be concerned.

'Why's that?' I asked.

There had been a problem over a rejected business offer, a moneymaking proposal that had been turned down. It led to upset and I was told that the lad who was with Frank the night he died is now long gone.

I didn't inquire further.

I learned at my nan's knee not to ask too many questions.

CHAPTER TWENTY
DREAMLAND

"'The time has come," the Walrus said,
"To talk of many things:
Of shoes – and ships – and sealing-wax –
Of cabbages – and kings –
And why the sea is boiling hot –
And whether pigs have wings."'

LEWIS CARROLL,

ALICE THROUGH THE LOOKING GLASS, 1871

The electric Warrior Wagon Frank bought that weekend when he first got out of prison is in his son's Wendy house now. He got over the novelty of it quickly, but it needs a little care. One of the big tyres has gone. Lyon the dog chewed it. He enjoyed his weird feast but it left the car off balance, wobbly.

Which I can still be.

If I've talked to Mum and maybe to my dad, wherever he is in the world, and Lara and young Frank are tucked into bed, I can mostly get off to sleep easily. I'm so tired anyway, knocked out. I try to get to the gym every day and I like to clean the house from top to bottom. I like clean.

But you can't stop the tricks of the brain, or the actions of things we don't understand.

Sometimes in the night I feel a chill like the night Frank died but it's probably more the breeze coming across the Irish Sea than any supernatural blarney drifting over.

We're all the architects of our own dream houses. My dread arrives in my sleep. The dream always begins and ends in the same way.

I'm running hand in hand with Dad through a mirrored airport terminal with images of us duplicated all around me.

The crowd of armed police chasing us gets bigger and bigger as we spring for a hazy horizon. The cops are shouting, screaming like sirens: 'Stop! We will shoot you.'

I hold Dad's hand tighter and we keep going, keep running from the men with waving guns towards a nothingness.

Dad turns his face to me. His hand slips out of mine. I stop running and cops are all over us. I'm handcuffed and shackled and I can see Dad running but now I don't know where he's going. There's a big jet ahead of him. The cops are shouting 'Shoot him' and he's not going to reach the plane on time. He's a moving but easy target. I scream at him to stop and put his hands up, to surrender.

There's no surrender. They hose him with bullets and take him down. Everything freezes. People are looking at Dad lying face down in his own blood. I break free and throw off my shackles and run to him. I bend down, take him in my arms ...

And then I wake up.

To a reality from which I know there can never be unrestricted freedom.

POSTSCRIPT
GUN LAW

'Freedom's just another word for nothin' left to lose.'

KRIS KRISTOFFERSON AND FRED FOSTER,
'ME AND BOBBY MCGEE', 1970

It was on 21 September 2009, ten days after Lara's coming-of-age party, that the dream turned into a nightmare. The past hammered on my front door.

The weekend had been one of tears and fears. Mum had been for medical tests and the news was not good. She had cancer in her bones and the doctors were not sure how serious it was but the prognosis was not good. It would, as always, take time and more tests to know the full story and how they and we could deal with it.

I was in total anguish. My mum? She'd always been there for me, always around to pick up the pieces, patch my life back together again. She's suffered before when I was in prison, and now, when our lives seemed to be settling down, this happened.

I'd been on the phone to her on the Monday morning and we were planning to meet that afternoon, but then I saw two men outside the house. In a moment they were at the door. The police. Two officers from Preston. They came in and sat down on the sofa opposite me.

The Italian *Ministero della Giustizia* had requested my extradition. They wanted me to complete my sentence – four years, eight months and eight days in jail.

My legs turned to jelly. Mum! Lara! Frank! Please God, not now.

I'd been released on a technicality but I'd been living openly and innocently for more than a decade in England and no one had bothered us. In 2007 my sentences effectively ran out. But legally, I didn't know. I've got an arrest warrant against me in Italy. If I set foot in the country, could I be arrested to serve the end of my time?

Trevor Colebourne, my solicitor, and I had calculated, with everything taken into account, that I'd have six months more to serve. That's with everything going well – but it's never like that, never simple, in Italy. Trevor deals a lot with extradition and human rights and says it's against the law for them, after all this time, to arrest me again: 'It's through their fault you were released. They knew you were a British national. You've not lived in hiding. You've got a National Insurance number, you're on benefits. Somebody could click a button and they can find you straight away. How can they arrest you after all these years, when you've done absolutely nothing wrong? You've got three points on your licence and that's it. How can they justify coming to re-arrest you for extradition for something you've already done time for? There is no judge in this land who would allow them to get away with that.'

I was wanted in my maiden name, as Marisa Di Giovine. My passport says Marisa Merico. But arresting me in England and in Italy means we're talking in two languages again.

The Preston officers, acting on the request of the London-based Serious Organised Crime Agency, were very pleasant. They noted my circumstances, my responsibilities for Frank and Lara, and I told them about my mum's cancer. They didn't arrest me on the spot. I surrendered my passport and they said I'd be given a date to appear in extradition court in London as soon as possible.

It was like the atom bomb had gone off inside my head. My thoughts were all over the place. I wasn't worried about myself – I'd do the time if I had to. Or even Lara, who is eighteen now and a strong girl. But Frank is just about to turn nine years old. Would I be free for his birthday on 21 October? And Mum? How would she cope? God, this was so unfair on her.

I was in turmoil – and then that other part of me, my stronger personality, took over and I began making arrangements. First, to fight the extradition warrant, and then to ensure my family would be safe if I was sent back to Italy and to jail.

I was straight with young Frank – I didn't want to be carted off in handcuffs without him being warned. No matter how absurd everyone told me the situation was, I was the one who had suffered it before and I knew anything could happen. So I told Frank I might have to go away but assured him he would be safe. My assurances didn't stop his tears or his anguish, and with every tear he cried, my heartbreak became more and more. You think you're going insane when you consider the prospect of your child being taken from you; it makes your mind rattle.

Lara and I were able to speak more freely about it. But it was one thing bang after the other. The day in 2009 when the Preston police came to my front door, Bruno was finally being released from prison in Italy. He is a proper free man now. Lara was happy for her dad but shaking her head at what was going on around her:

'After seventeen years – just about all my life – my dad's out of prison and I have him back, I can see him in the open air. At the same time they're trying to take my mum away from me. What is happening?'

I could understand her confusion. It was a mess. But one I couldn't clean up myself. I had to work with the system. It wasn't comforting. When we studied the paperwork being delivered from the Italian authorities – the European arrest warrant described me as a Mafia operator in the 1970s, when I would have been little more than a toddler – it was hard to comprehend, and hard not to laugh. They'd got their paperwork wrong and the dates were all askew. But no matter how silly some of it seemed, I knew just how very serious the situation was.

There's not much more terrifying than faceless bureaucracy.

On 1 October 2009 I arrived at Westminster Magistrates Court in Horseferry Road, London, wheeling my overnight bag. Trevor Colebourne had travelled south on the early morning train but I didn't want to risk not being on time so I stayed in a cheap hotel near the court the night before. It was very much a formality but my nerves were jangling. The main reception area was quiet, people just whispering to each other, and I was taken into a side room by Trevor and a tall detective. I was officially arrested but not taken to the cells. Instead we went directly into a brightly lit, modern courtroom to hear if they would lock me up to wait for a decision on the extradition or whether I could get bail.

The police were not opposed to me being free and suggested ideas like me checking in from my home phone to show that I had not skipped the country. And to give up Frank's passport as well as my own. They knew me well enough to know I'd never leave the kids behind.

I was sitting at the back of the court when the magistrate ordered me into the dock. I looked around, a little lost. At first, I was also lost for words and could hardly confirm my identity, my name. I couldn't hear my voice as I spoke.

But I clearly heard the lawyer acting for the Italian authorities say that I had four years, eight months and eight days of my sentence to run; there was no mention of my time spent in Durham or Italy. The girl from the Crown Prosecution Service didn't push too hard, although she said the charges involved narcotics trafficking. Legally, it was a mishmash of technicalities and precedent and of the time that had elapsed.

I also had to think about what might happen to me in the Italian prison system. I'm the Mafia Princess, the daughter of a man giving testimony against organised crime families. Genuinely, there was every reason to believe that I might be murdered in jail just to get at my dad.

Trevor explained that my case was unique – 'I've never known of such circumstances before' – and as he talked it did seem ludicrous that there was even a remote chance of me being extradited.

I knew better. It had happened to me before. I put the odds at 50–50. Still, I'd have to wait till 20 October when the full extradition hearing was to begin. Then, within days of the international paperwork starting to land on Trevor's desk, it became clear that date would come and go. It had to be postponed into nearly December 2009. And after that, postponed again.

There was a London hearing in January 2010 and a couple of weeks later another appearance, which I can only call a cameo, at Westminster Court. Each time I was up and down the country by train, not knowing if I'd be going back to Lara and Frank.

Then, in early 2010, it started in Italy. Dad was knocked down in a hit-and-run incident just before he was due to give evidence in a case involving one of the international arms dealers from his past. The case involved the dumping of toxic waste and had the potential to be extremely embarrassing for the influential people involved.

Immediately afterwards, the offices in Calabria where Mafia investigations were being co-ordinated were firebombed. My aunt's bar there was attacked. A very violent message was being sent, and it wasn't hard for anyone to understand. Especially me.

I became really paranoid. I had an alarm system installed in the house. I'm careful and I watch who is around, but it is in Italy that I know there is most chance of paying for my father's new life with my own.

In the extradition courts I believe I wasn't just fighting to stay in England with my children and mother, I was fighting for my own survival. I knew I was strong enough to fight, for I have much to hold on to, but in the early hours of the night I would sometimes lie there and wonder. In 2010 I'd been back in Britain for more than a dozen years. Would it be another dozen before I'd be truly free?

Will I ever escape my life with the Mafia, a life I was born into, bonded to by love, and for which I've been paying for such a long time?

Will I end up paying the ultimate price?

But, even alone in the dark of the night, I know I will come through. I have got this far. I am a survivor.

They say life begins at forty. I hit that landmark at the start of 2010 and I plan to attack the rest of my time with a ferocious intent. No matter what happens to me, or what the future holds.

As the extradition horror invaded my life, I received first-hand evidence that our family's 21st-century Mafia genera-tion is firmly established. A group of teenagers and kids in their early twenties from our family visited Nan on the Piazza Preapli. They were not there to offer condolences about her failing health or her imminent demise. They were there to talk about the death of my dad and my Auntie Rita.

They were to be killed for providing evidence to the authorities. My dad's brothers were also going to be wiped out, not, it seemed, for any offence other than being related to Dad.

Not long ago these punks would have risked death and certainly punishment simply for turning up unannounced. Now they arrived with threats. The word on the streets of Milan is that a territorial battle, something big, is going to happen.

The intelligence says there is something or someone behind the threats, not just a bunch of wannabe *Mafiosa*. But the youngsters are the ones carrying the weapons. I learned one vital lesson from my life in the Mafia and it's that the real power is in the hands of the gunmen.

And once again they are on our doorstep, the new gun-toting generation of the Serraino–Di Giovine clan, putting a family at war.

By 2010 the 'Ndrangheta had overtaken the Cosa Nostra as Europe's most powerful Mafia organisation. The influence may still come from the South, from Calabria, but the action is going on in Milan.

The 'Ndrangheta's power infiltrates the catwalks, the fashion industry as pressured as the governing bodies of the city's other big crowd-pleaser, the soccer teams, who are regularly urged to be generous with their profits.

At present the Mafia are eyeing up a fifteen billion euro government investment fund aimed at helping Milan prepare a proper welcome for the Expo World Fair in 2015. It's not if, but how much of that cash will go into the Mafia coffers. In the second decade of the 21st century the 'Ndrangheta has an annual turnover of £30 billion. It supplies at least 85 per cent of the cocaine in Europe. Like Dad before them, they have cut out the middlemen. The 'Ndrangheta buy direct from Colombia at a cost of 1,000 euros a kilo, which is sold on the streets at a rate of 30,000 euros a kilo. They're snorting all the way to the bank. And the profits are being invested in legitimate businesses across the North of Italy. There are high-level board meetings about the corporate plans every working day.

But, as I said, the action may be in the North but the historic methods still resonate from the land of the orange blossom. It doesn't matter when or where or whom – if something or someone gets in the way, it's dealt with the old-fashioned way.

That became evident outside a pizza parlour in the German town of Duisburg in 2007. It's no coincidence that Duisburg boasts the world's biggest inland harbour. A good asset for import and export.

When two 'Ndrangheta clans feuded over who ran the harbour, the Pelle–Romeo family won control. They executed six of the opposition Nirta–Strangio family outside the pizza palace. It was a classic shoot-and-run operation.

There have been no arrests.

People ask me if the influence and lethal power of the Mafia will ever end. From what I've lived through I suspect that's unlikely. Control is the key, and attitude determines how it is applied. The Mafia say: *Ser vo mortu lo to nemicu, nun fari scrusciu* [If you kill your enemy, he can't make any noise]. It's not a life-affirming motto.

I've turned my back on all that, for that's not how I see my future or the future of my kids. Life should be celebrated, not destroyed. The two things I'm proud of in my life so far – and I've much to be sorry about – are Lara and Frank. They're my achievement. Our love is everything.

As it says at the beginning, this book is for them.

ACKNOWLEDGEMENTS

I want to thank all the people who have helped me to reach a place where I've been able to tell my story with complete honesty: not just the professionals who have been supportive and kind but all those who have been so much part of my life. I send my love to them all.

My mum and dad: Mum, it's only now I know exactly how much you mean to me. I'm sorry for all the hurt I've caused. Dad, I've always loved you even when I shouldn't have. You'll always be my father; if at times I've not liked you, I never stopped loving you.

Frank and Lara: the love I have for you both is like no other. You are the truly pure and innocent results from my life, my achievements. Look after each other always.

Bruno: for our young love and giving me our beautiful daughter Lara. My nan in Italy, no matter what, I love you.

Vera: a lovely, caring lady who has taken me in her arms as if I were her own daughter.

Tracy: who listened to me a million times over during the past ten years and helped me through my darkest moments.

Sue: you helped me through prison life, gave me hope, love and affection; you were like a mum to me.

Naima: you have been like a sister, always there for me.

Ashley: you helped me find my real self once again. Thank you for being there when it mattered.

Uncle John: I truly appreciate all you've done for young Frank through the years.

Maxine and the Barns family: for making me laugh even when I wanted to cry. Rachael and family and Johanna for caring. My aunties and uncles and all the others who have also cared so much.

The special people who I've lost: my Auntie Eileen, my English nan and grandad, my Italian granddad and, of course, Frank Senior. He was a tormented soul on earth and is hopefully at peace in Heaven. He might have done bad things but he was a good person and they say the good die young. Out of our love came our precious son and for that I will be for ever thankful.

This book is the result of marvellous team work:

I want to thank Douglas Thompson for his expertise, advice and caring, and Lesley and Dandy for their kindness and hospitality; also Amanda Stocks at Exclusive Press & Publicity, Diane Banks at Diane Banks Associates Literary Agency and Nick Owens. I owe great thanks to Susanna Abbott at Harper-Collins for giving me the opportunity to tell the truth at last.

And to my solicitor Trevor Colebourne, who knows me as well as he does the law and deals with heartache and legal headaches with equal calm and an acute level of under-standing of the difficult process of both.